TO KNOW WE'RE LOVED

A TIME TO LOVE
AND
A TIME TO DIE

The aim of CONSCIOUSNESS CLASSICS is to bring to life
significant publications in the consciousness field, which have
not been available, and to showcase new books which are
destined to become classics.

CONSCIOUSNESS CLASSICS conserves these texts as the authors
originally intended them, in a carefully re-designed
contemporary format for new generations of readers.
These books are an important legacy of groundbreaking
consciousness explorers of the 20th century.

RESHAD FEILD

TO KNOW
WE'RE LOVED

A TIME TO LOVE
AND
A TIME TO DIE

GATEWAYS BOOKS AND TAPES
NEVADA CITY, CALIFORNIA

Gateways Books and Tapes
P.O. Box 370
Nevada City, CA 95959
1-800-869-0658
http://www.gatewaysbooksandtapes.com

Previously published under the title: *The Invisible Way*

First published in Great Britain 1979, by Element Books Ltd.
First published in the USA 1993 by Element, Inc.
First published in Australia 1993 by Element Books Ltd. for Jacaranda Wiley Limited

Book design by iTRANSmedia
Cover art: Matthias Schossig, photo © 2004 by Christian Nowak

 Library of Congress Cataloging-in-Publication Data

Feild, Reshad.
  To know we're loved : a time to love and a time to die / Reshad
Feild.-- Gateways consciousness classics ed.
     p. cm.
Originally published: The invisible way. Rockport, Mass. : Element, 1994.
  ISBN 0-89556-154-9
  1. Sufisim--Prayer-books and devotions--English. I. Title.
  BP189.62.F44 2004
  297.4'4--dc22
                        2003026200

ISBN: 0-89556-154-9

This book is dedicated to my wife, Barbara Feild, and my family, and to all those with whom I have shared this journey over the past forty years.

Because I love
There is an invisible way across the sky,
Birds travel by that way, the sun and moon
And all the stars travel that path by night.

Because I love
There is a river flowing all night long.

Because I love
All night the river flows into my sleep,
Ten thousand things are sleeping in my arms,
And sleeping wake, and flowing are at rest.

KATHLEEN RAINE

FOREWORD
BY COLEMAN BARKS

Rumi says, "Inside a lover's heart there's another world, and yet another." *To Know We're Loved* tracks Reshad Feild's evolving love story through several more openings past his previous work *The Last Barrier*. There are worlds within this phenomenal world we inhabit and there is even agreement, more or less, on how it proceeds. Such figures as William Blake, the Jesus of the *Gospel of Thomas*, Rumi, 'Ibn Árabi, Kathleen Raine, and Reshad himself explore the shifts of attention that explain this layering. Reshad quotes them all as he shows us how the flow of spirit feels *in the moment*. He jogs us awake to those simultaneous events and to how the recognition of them becomes part of us. We *do* live in at least two worlds at once.

In this book, more than in *The Last Barrier*, Reshad celebrates the many levels of the feminine—Sophie, Elizabeth, Nur. There are wonderful scenes: a Stonehenge morning, Sophie's singing restaurant. Within them we develop an inner sensing, the intuition that knows the mysteries often associated with the feminine. What mysteries? How patience is the key to will. What it is to "die consciously" and the subtleties of "the mother's breath," 7-1-7-1-7. Reshad's world is full of possibility, sudden knowing, and profound enigmas, not the least of which is the love story that carries the narrative along. "Sentiment and love are enemies," he says at the end here, a startlingly revolutionary sentence! Try expounding that to the mass-mind movie culture. "The journey of the soul on the path of return is not a sentimental journey," he reminds us. Keep this book near, along with *The Last Barrier*, and reread the passages you've marked.

COLEMAN BARKS
Spring, 2002
Georgia, U.S.A.

Poet Coleman Barks is today's foremost interpreter of the poet Rumi. His works include *The Soul of Rumi* and *The Essential Rumi*.

PROLOGUE

I had been asked to write a new introduction to this new edition of the book that was originally called *The Invisible Way*, the sequel to the first part of the trilogy, *The Last Barrier*. I tried again and again to compose something which would bring the book up-to-date since it was originally published in 1979. However I realized that what I have already said holds true to this day, and there is really nothing to add!

I was a young man when I wrote the story in this book, and now I am in my 70th year, and still living like a gypsy. I do not travel as much as I used to in the old days, but continue to write and give the teachings of The Inner Path, wherever I am. I thank all those thousands of people I have had the honor to meet on this long journey throughout the world, and who have helped me have the courage and perseverance to continue to this day....

RESHAD FEILD

June 8th, 2003
Zug, Switzerland

PROLOGUE TO THE FIRST EDITION

The subject of time will never cease to amaze me. Over the years, so much has happened in my life that its course seems in retrospect to have been relentless and certain, however much I may have thought otherwise. Destiny had its part to play. Often I tried to escape it and instead put myself in the hands of fate, finding myself swept along with a stream of sleep-walkers who never really inhabited this world nor saw its exquisite beauty. It was only when life became increasingly painful, and my own stupidity obvious, that I was finally able to surrender to a force much greater than myself. It was a living experiment for which I forfeited my own personal life, or what I thought it was, for an uncertain outcome that has become the only possible way to live.

Destiny reaches out beckoning, and the circumstances of life become a trial of a human being's capacity to share consciously in the evolution of humanity. Preparation and capacity are necessary to heed the voice, to take a plunge into the unknown, to surrender ourselves to Love itself. If we hesitate too long, we become lost in the mind's labyrinth—the lamp of knowledge that guides us through the dangers of human ignorance and personal willfulness goes out.

Not many are prepared to conduct this experiment, for Love requires of us complete sacrifice, even the final sacrifice of suffering. Yet the paradox of it all is that sooner or later, even if only at the end of our lives, we will all be confronted with the knowledge that "reason is powerless in the expression of Love" and that only through dying to the illusion of ourselves as separate from the One Reality can we find life.

This book is a love story—about love that faces death. To truly know and accept that this body dies, and that this is the only time that we have, is the most powerful weapon we can ever have. With this understanding, we can begin to live passionately, not wasting a moment of the precious time that is allocated to us, plunging gratefully into the immediacy of living. We work now, for the future of humanity, and, as we know we are loved, time will be on our side.

RESHAD FEILD

December 2, 1978
Vancouver, Canada

1

The challenge that life affords us, faced honestly, takes us into many and varied situations. One of the most important periods of my life was spent traveling in and out of Turkey. I had gone there to study with the whirling dervishes and had met a man who became my spiritual teacher. Over the years, I traveled to many countries of the world, from the Far East through India to Pakistan and then high up into the northern provinces of Gilgit and Chitral. Like many others, I was searching for a real purpose, attempting to unveil the essential reality of life.

The time I spent in Turkey was so rich that I found it hard to relate my experiences to everyday life when I returned to London. My mind kept taking me back to the situation where it had been given a taste of something greater than what I had normally seen and encountered in a western culture. I realized that my task was to try to put into practice what I had learned. But after the initial flush of enthusiasm I found the depth of my understanding remarkably shallow. It was one of the most difficult periods of my life. Yet, despite the sense of separation and loss that I experienced when I left Turkey, a relentless force kept me going.

It is not a negative thing to realize how little we know. It was a profound experience that granted certain energy that was not available before. It pushed me to ask an inner question day after day, leading on to more and more opportunities for understanding. I realized that the spiritual way was not an escape but a journey into life. The truths I had experienced, once tested carefully, were found to apply wherever I went and in whatever circumstances. How could it be otherwise if what I had seen and known was real? Perhaps it was with this in mind that my teacher had given me certain tasks to fulfill after leaving Turkey, the last of which sent me to Mexico.

It was the monsoon season, the dirt roads ran with mud, and the scorpions, sheltering from the rain, came into the house. I was staying in an extraordinary village called Tepoztlan, just south of Mexico City. Its history goes back to Aztec times, and in the surrounding hills people still speak Navhatl, the ancient language. The village is dominated by high mountains, where a pyramid is dedicated to Tepozteco, the Aztec god of the wind. It is a place of great beauty, yet there was an uneasy undercurrent of a hidden and primitive world of magic.

I had set up a small group in Tepoztlan, as I had been instructed. It was an experiment to see if a dedicated group of people could learn to live together and to draw to themselves the teaching needed in the moment. All were to varying degrees familiar with the ideas that there are worlds within the phenomenal one we normally see. Many members of our group, in fact, were psychologists or philosophy students. They had found that remnants of an enduring knowledge of these other worlds were known and practiced in some of the more outlying villages in Mexico and, indeed, throughout the whole South American Continent.

I was confronted with this when I climbed the mountain to the pyramid at sunrise one morning soon after I had arrived. I had been warned not to go alone as stories were circulated locally about people who had been swept off the steep path by a fierce wind appearing from nowhere as they neared the summit. I had discounted the story as superstition and ignored the advice.

One hundred feet below the top of the mountain, an iron grill closes a narrow gap in the cliff face that must be passed to finally reach the pyramid. It was locked at night, but the caretaker was usually there before dawn. On this occasion, however, with the sun just breaking over the mountains, I found the gate still padlocked and no sign of the man.

I sat down tired and disappointed. For no particular reason, I felt an overwhelming fear begin to creep over me. And then the wind started. It curled around my legs and swirled across the rock face, raising huge columns of dust. I experienced an incredible sensation of being drawn off the path, away from the protection of the mountain behind, and over the cliff. It took every ounce of my will not to succumb to the elemental power unleashed at that moment. I wedged myself into the rocks and braced my legs against the roots of a tree. Above me, I could hear the echoes of the wind roaring through the iron grill.

Eventually the wind calmed, and by the time I had recovered sufficiently to start down the mountain the sun was well up in the sky. Halfway down, I met the caretaker coming up the path. He apologized. His wife and two daughters had suddenly become ill, and he had been afraid to leave them, though one hour later the sickness had gone.

I was very thoughtful as I climbed down the path. I explained it all as a freak encounter with natural causes but I was unsatisfied, and it became clear that I had perhaps been a bit naïve. If I had any doubt it was soon dissipated a few nights afterwards during a regular evening meeting with the small group that had invited me to Mexico.

The rain battered on the roof of the house and poured down the walls into the street. Without any warning I was suddenly aware of flames outside the window. Two of the group immediately went out to see what was happening. As they rounded the corner, they were just in time to catch a glimpse of two men running into the darkness. Sheets of flame illuminated the back wall. Below was a small charcoal burner called a *veladura*, on which four white eggs were burning rapidly in a bed of grasses and herbs. Kerosene had obviously been poured over them and set on fire.

The flames were quickly extinguished, and we resumed our discussion. But there was something in the atmosphere; we felt uneasy, and it was impossible to concentrate. I could not sleep that night. In the morning, I visited a friend who had lived in that area for many years to ask his advice. When I told him the story, he too was concerned.

"This is an extremely serious matter," he said. "You must never underestimate the power of these people. They appear primitive, it is true, but the shamans here carry knowledge that has been handed down by word of mouth for thousands of years. It seems that you have intruded on their space, and so they have taken action. You had better go immediately to Mexico City where I know someone you should see."

"Surely it is not as serious as that?" I asked. "I mean, burning four eggs cannot do any real harm, can it? And anyway I'm leaving for California in two days."

"Do as I say, I beg you," he replied. "Stop on your way north. It can only do good, and you would be a fool to ignore the signs. The local magicians believe that the true shape of living things can be found in the egg, and the use of eggs in healing and magic is well known here."

I had heard of this before, in my studies of esoteric healing among the Druids in England, and I was well versed with the axiom "As above, so below" with all things in nature. Moreover, when my teacher had explained the unorthodox and powerful healing of a man I had known in north London several years before, he had spoken of the egg as a symbol of the invisible matrix from which creation is continuously becoming.

The man in that instance had suffered suicidal fits of depression for many years and had been instructed to keep a white egg with him for 24 hours before our visit. The egg had then been taken from him; inscribed carefully with a prayer; and broken over the man's head. He had been healed in due course but when I had asked for an explanation of why such a method had been necessary my teacher had said that the operation was as much for me as it was for the man who was healed. "The answer lies in the egg," he had said enigmatically, "and remember I know what attracts them."

Years later when I had seen enough of these recoveries I understood what he had been driving at; that attraction to such phenomena is a limitation in the way of truth.

Nothing now would have induced me to get involved with this "healing" in Mexico City, but my friend insisted. I spent a little time trying to convince both him and myself that there was really no need to do anything; finally I agreed to go and see the healer he had recommended. The directions were written out and I was told to be at the house on the outskirts of Mexico City before dawn, as there was no phone and people had been known to wait in line for over eight hours. As with the healing in London, I was to bring a white egg I had carried with me for twenty-four hours before going.

I persuaded an Israeli friend of mine who lived in the city to drive me out to the address I had been given. Samuel was an unlikely person to ask as he was totally uninterested in healing or psychism of any sort, completely orthodox in his upbringing and actively involved in the Jewish community in Mexico City. It took a lot of persuading, but finally, as a joke, he said that he would come with me.

"Why don't you bring an egg as well?" I asked. "I mean, we could all do with a bit of healing somewhere. . . ."

The next morning, before dawn, we set off in his car, armed with our white eggs. Samuel had his on his lap, and I held mine in my hand. Just before reaching our destination I shook the egg I was holding.

"Samuel," I said, "there is something odd here. My egg is rattling inside."

"Don't be ridiculous," he said. Holding his egg up to his ear, he paused. "I don't believe it! So is mine."

As the first light broke over Mexico City, we drove past the grounds of an oil refinery and entered a narrow street. Clouds of steam bellowed through gratings in the dirt road and curled up into the dawn shadows.

We knocked on the door of the house we had been directed to. Almost immediately it was opened by a man who greeted us in Spanish. "Come in," he said graciously. "You must be the one who is going to Los Angeles tomorrow. I will see that you will not have to wait more than forty-five minutes." I was startled by his statement as I had not told him this and there was no other way he could have known.

He ushered us in but it was dark inside and it took some time to adjust to the low lighting as we came through the door. All our misgivings were brushed aside, however, as our attention was riveted on what we could now see. We were standing in a thirty-five foot long passageway. On both sides of the corridor men, women, and children were waiting, crowded together in a space so narrow that even with our backs firmly pressed to the wall behind

4

there was barely room to get by the person standing opposite. As I looked around, I noticed that each person had a white egg in his or her hands.

At the far end of the passage, a curtain separated the healer from the crowd outside. The sound of continuous murmuring could be heard. It sounded something like "Lord Jesus Christ, may I be allowed to take on the sins of this person; may the poison come into the egg."

I nudged Samuel firmly in the ribs, "Do you see what I see?" I whispered. But his glasses had steamed up and it was unlikely that he could see anything. "Look at the birds!" In the rush of impressions from the crowd of people in the hallway, I had not noticed until that moment that the walls were lined with bird cages. Dozens of small birds were singing and chattering, while birdseed and feathers fluttered down onto the heads of the people below. I counted thirty-eight cages in all.

Samuel took off his glasses and wiped them carefully. "God knows what on earth we are doing here," he said "and me Jewish, too!"

The man who had let us in came for us as he had promised. Taking me by the hand, he led us through the crowd towards the curtain at the end of the passage. I noticed that many people were silently praying, and others were fingering their rosaries. In the half-light of the passageway, the white eggs stood out like beacons.

We were told to wait outside for a few moments. Then our guide came out once more and we entered the little sanctuary. I am not sure what hit me first, the ageless beauty of the woman who stood in front of me or the weird conglomeration of objects around the room. The air was thick with a traditional Mexican incense made from the sap of the copal tree. Through the smoke, I could see a series of shelves lined with glasses half-filled with water. In each one, an egg had been broken. But they were not normal eggs. Some were a slimy green, some black, some cloudy, and despite the incense there was a terrible smell of decay. On my left was a table bearing a cross, a cheap plastic Buddha painted gold, a stuffed rattlesnake, and a stuffed baby alligator. The walls were covered with pictures of Christ, but none of the Virgin Mary. I could feel Samuel shaking.

"Give her the egg," the man said. He was standing next to Samuel, and I was definitely relieved that I had not had to go first!

Samuel handed the woman his egg. I could not take my eyes off her. She could have been anywhere from forty to seventy-five years old. Her face was completely pure and devoid of any personality. In fact, she seemed almost sexless. She took Samuel's egg from his hand and without any introduction started chanting again while rubbing the egg all round his body. She did not actually touch him but appeared to work about an inch away from him, as if she were rolling out pastry. Then, she spun him around, continued over the back of his body from the head down to the feet, made the sign of the cross on his back, and turned him to face her once more. Picking up a glass half-filled with water from a table beside her, she broke the egg into the glass.

Neither Samuel nor I could speak. Out of the eggshell came a few drops of yolk, a heaped teaspoonful of what turned out to be salt, and a large quantity of black ash. Shaking her head, she turned to us and said, "This is not good at all, and if you do not get this cleared up you could be very sick. You must come back here each week for six more weeks, and then it will be clear. The salt represents envy. You have many people who do not like you and are envious of you. It is shown here. The ash represents the pain that you have been through in your life." Then she put the glass on the shelf with the others and turned to me.

I would have liked to have been anywhere else in the world at that moment! I had seen the egg treatment before, and I had no desire to see it again, particularly perpetrated on myself. However, there was no way out. I handed her my egg and opened myself to the Highest Source while she went through the same procedure as with Samuel. While she did, I had an unusual sensation of floating, I couldn't be sure if my feet were actually on the ground or not.

When she broke the egg into a glass, what came out of my egg made her start back. "*Muy malo, muy malo*," she said. "Very bad, very bad. Someone has tried to kill you. Look!"

Very carefully she tipped the contents of the egg into the glass. There were a few drops of yolk, and then a perfect miniature replica of a charcoal burner slid into the water, followed by a mass of black ash. I was shocked and decided at that moment my fascination for the elemental world of magic had gone far enough.

"They have used the eggs," she said. "Look, do you see the candle sticking out of the *veladura*? It represents the concentration of thought they have used against you and the fire that they must have lit. This is very bad, *muy malo*. I will have to do special work for you but as you cannot come back each week if you are going away to Los Angeles, then your friend here will come back with the photograph of you. It will be the same."

With that she took the glass and put it in a special place at the back of the room, and we left, squeezing our way through the crowd and brushing the birdseed from our heads as we went. The daylight was a blessed relief.

"It was a trick," Samuel started off, Samuel, the incorrigible skeptic. "She must have palmed another egg or something. The whole thing is ridiculous."

"But what about the miniature charcoal burner?" I replied. "You cannot deny that it was there. How could she have known what happened in Tepoztlan? And what was all that salt and ash in your egg?"

We argued all the way back to his flat, but with all the drama of the event there was so much humor in it that, instead of coming to blows, we ended up laughing until the tears ran down our faces. After all, what was an Israeli who had fought in three wars—and presumably that was the pain and suffering that had been picked up in the ash—and a former English antique dealer doing in a situation like this? The whole thing was ludicrous, but finally Samuel agreed to go back with my photograph.

The following week I telephoned him from Los Angeles to ask what had happened.

"Your egg was full of black oil," he said.

"What does that mean?" I asked.

"She said that it was better than last week and that it was a start." I could almost see him shrug his shoulders.

Six weeks later, Samuel called me to say that at long last the egg she had been using over my photograph was clean.

When my business was completed in Los Angeles, I returned to my small flat and routine life in London. I had learned much from the experience in Mexico, particularly that we are given similar situations until we learn to redeem them by being awake to the inner meaning of the experience and not to its appearance alone. We write our own book in life. The incident with the egg was just the way I needed to experience something at the time. I worked hard to assimilate all that had transpired, yet there was still old business, lingering situations as yet unfulfilled within myself.

My teacher and I had not communicated with each other since our last meeting over two and a half years before. "You have your own inner guide now," he had said. "So it is a time to trust and put into practice what you have learned." I found it difficult to live the life that I could perceive but that was so hard to express in the material world.

Eventually it became obvious that I needed to return to Turkey to complete a cycle. I wished to go back once more to Konya, a city in Anatolia, where something of an unconditional Love had been granted to me in an experience that I could not forget. In the six months since my return from Mexico, I had managed to get my personal life in order, so that it had become possible to leave England and pursue my spiritual training.

I wrote to my friend and teacher in Turkey, explaining completely and honestly that I did not know what the next step of my life was to be, nor what I was meant to do at that time. I spoke of the loneliness of separation from him, of the difficulties I had been experiencing and I asked him to see me again. I did not know exactly where he was living, but I did have a forwarding address in Turkey. I felt certain that the letter would reach him, and I no longer doubted that there would be a way opened if it was destined. I was beginning to realize that in this pursuit there is no such thing as chance.

2

The dun-coloured plains of Anatolia were broken only by the sky and the hills to the north. I could just make out the city of Konya from the air. Known in biblical times as the ancient Iconium, Konya had been a centre of trade and learning for nearly a millennium. It was also the home of Mevlana Jalalu'ddin Rumi, who was one of the greatest Sufi poets and mystics who ever lived. He is often called the Pole of Love since his knowledge of Universal Love, like the philosopher's stone, brought the possibility for the knowledge of completion beyond form. It was and is all embracing to anyone of any religious background. Thus, Mevlana Jalalu'ddin Rumi was held in equal esteem by those from many diverse spiritual and philosophical traditions during his lifetime over 700 years ago, and I speculated that, since this is a time for the understanding of the unity of religious ideals, perhaps Konya would become a place of pilgrimage for all those seeking to understand the basic truth underlying all religious and all human aspiration.

It was a twenty-minute bus ride from the airstrip, and I looked forward to the first houses and minarets that would signal the outskirts of Konya. Later would come the pedicabs, horse carts, taxis, buses, handcarts, and pedestrians. I could almost memorize the route through the modern section of the city to the ruins of the Seljuk *medreses*, or libraries, and finally the major street, the Mevlana Caddesi, which led to the tomb and museum of Mevlana.

It is very hard to put into words the deep sense of awe that Konya inspires in me and still harder to talk about the feelings I experienced sitting in my hotel room as I prepared to greet my friend and teacher once again. It was difficult not to be in a state of expectation. I had been taught that nothing can ever be as we anticipate. There is always something greater than we have imagined, and things do not always work out as we would wish them.

I had risen while it was still dark. After bathing, I sat by the window, where I could just see the square by the museum and the mosque opposite. The dawn was touching the sky behind. "*Allahu Akbar, Allahu Akbar.* God is Great,

God is Great." The call to prayer had begun. Each mosque burst forth its cry to the faithful to come to prayer. I watched as the last person hurried into the mosque. Only the street sounds outside remained. As I prepared to leave the room, the telephone rang. "Your friend is here," the concierge said. "He says to come down and join him for coffee."

My teacher hadn't changed at all during those years, and I experienced the same love and warmth as the first day I met him in the shop in London. We embraced somewhat formally, and he motioned me to join him at a table. Two cups of Turkish coffee were already there.

"It has been a long time," he began, smiling. "How are you? How have you spent these years? All I know is second-hand, and that it has not been easy for you."

I remembered how he had put me through test after test, presumably, to see whether I was capable and persevering enough to continue. I thought of the endless and apparently pointless experiences that I had found myself in and of the joy and the pain that seemed to balance one another out.

"Did you go to Mexico as you were instructed?" he asked. "You did not write, and I was worried, although I knew that you probably did not know how to get in touch with me. What happened there?"

I had to relate every detail: what I had done, whom I had met, and so on. I had seen him do this before, but this time there was a greater intensity in his questioning. When I told him about the egg story, he laughed. "But I said that the answer lies in the egg, did I not? I wonder if you have understood?" We were silent for a while. A waiter came and brought us more coffee.

"Now," he continued, "let's speak directly. You wrote to me and asked that you might come to see me again, but you did not say in your letter exactly why. I'm sure you must have some idea why you have come."

I did my best to phrase an answer. Finally, I explained that I did not have a specific reason that I could put into words. Somehow, I had assumed that everything would be made clear just by being with him again.

We spent a long time talking, over breakfast. It was typical of the Middle East: fresh bread, white goat cheese, black olives, and honey. My teacher asked me, again and again, for any details that he felt that I had not told him about my experiences in the last two years. Finally he said, "I do understand, and even perhaps sense some of the pain that you have been through, but I am sure you realize that without a real question in our hearts we cannot expect to receive a clear answer. So often in the past you just went along with whatever was going on, never daring to challenge events. What you learned was thus limited by this lack of clarity. But that was all right, since you lacked the experience to ask a real question. You simply tried to reinforce your own theories. It was really for this reason that I sent you back to a routine life in

England, so that you could perhaps assimilate something of what you were shown while we were together and thus be able to ask a question of real value. Does that make sense?"

"I think so," I answered. I was beginning to realize that the fulfilment of our new meeting would be in the quality of my own internal questioning and distillation of all that I had experienced since we had last met.

"Things have changed now," he went on. "You do have more experience, and I sense that there is a good reason why you are here." He touched my shoulder for a moment and smiled.

"Honestly," I said, "it seems impossible for me to phrase, in one sentence, all the questions I have had. There are so many, and there is so much doubt. To be honest with you, there is much that I am tired of—at least things that I have seen. So what about the egg? What if someone *can* produce from the inside of a chicken's egg the materialization of an event already past? What if an egg *is* broken on someone's head and the person *does* get better? Does all that really have anything to do with what I am pursuing? So much of what I thought I knew has turned out to be unreal. Now it is a question of not knowing which way to turn. That is why I have come to see you."

"You *thought* you knew . . . Ah! Almost always, if we think we know anything absolutely, we know nothing. We can know only minute portions of the true reality. We make mental concepts of the truth in its bare essence. Do you remember the wonderful saying in the tradition of the Sufis, 'If you see yourself in the mirror, then all you worship are your own thoughts; but if you see God in the mirror, then God is seeing himself in you?'"

We drank the rest of our coffee in silence, and then he turned the cups upside down on the saucer as I had seen him do many times before. It is a popular pastime in the Middle East as it is said that it is possible to read the potentiality of what lies in the moment in the pattern of the coffee grounds in the cup. "It's like the egg, isn't it?" he said, smiling.

Finally, I asked him what he saw in the coffee grounds. "Oh, it's not so bad, actually, if you can find the question."

He stood up then, suggesting that we visit the tombs of the great Sufi saints, which are in Konya. This was not a new experience for me. I knew when we turned up the main street from the hotel that we were going first to visit the tomb of Shems i Tabriz, the wandering dervish and Gnostic who had been the agent for the transformation of love within Mevlana Jalalu'ddin Rumi 700 years before. Shems was reputedly the greatest alchemist of his time, and his passionate desire was for friendship with one of those close to God. In Jalalu'ddin Rumi, he found the manifestation of his longing. Teachers, mentors and pupils to each other, each mirrored the love and knowledge of the Truth in the other. When Shems was finally killed by jealous disciples of Mevlana, the shock of separation caused such longing and refinement in the soul of Jalalu'ddin that on his death bed he was granted Union with God; at that moment there was no God but God.

We took our shoes off and washed at the fountain outside the mosque. We entered and walked quietly across the simple whitewashed room to the grill facing the entrance. Behind it was the tomb of Shems i Tabriz. Our prayers were silent, and we opened ourselves to the moment.

Lines of pilgrims were waiting in the garden when we came out into the chill dawn. Some were in tears; all were in prayer. We walked slowly towards the tomb of Mevlana. Neither of us spoke. My thoughts ran on; it was difficult not to recall all the times that I had visited Konya before and walked the same route. As always, my heart burned in the knowledge of the great love that had been expressed here. This burning led me to the conviction that the saints whose tombs we visited were not merely historical figures. Rather, through their sacrifice and surrender, they had come to exist in a world beyond time and space, and therefore beyond the divisive walls of religious form and belief.

I spoke of this to my teacher as we walked. "Let me put it to you this way," he answered. "When we have the courage to realize that life itself is the teacher, the timeless truth lying within the moment can come forth from the knowledge written in the great books and preserved at sacred places. The difficulty is that, traveling or studying books, including the sacred scriptures, is useless without your own inner experience."

"The major problem for Westerners," he went on, "is that they are always trying to copy the experiences of others. This is ridiculous. No one has ever experienced what another has felt. No one can ever feel another's joy or another's pain. People can think that they know, but thinking is a poor and perhaps unintelligent limitation of what lies within each of us. This probably sounds discouraging, particularly if you cannot face your own inner reality and must chase after another's, but it is true. It would be useful for you to understand this. Your experience is your own, and mine is my own."

"Then why is it," I asked him, "that so many people come back to Konya and to other places of pilgrimage, year after year? Does it mean that they have not learned the lesson?"

"Not quite," he replied. "It is rather like the ocean. You may learn to swim, but the ocean is continuously changing, and so, in a sense, the swimming is different. It adapts itself to the mood of the water. The ocean is the same, but its surface is always changing. Thus, when you visit someone like Mevlana, or Shems i Tabriz, or the city of Jerusalem, or Chartres Cathedral in France, for example, you are encountering something of such depth that, no matter how many times you go and however much you have understood, further realizations and deeper understandings are always possible.

"It is a question of unfolding. It will be necessary for you to meditate on this, for I am attempting to speak of things that really cannot be talked about. After all, there is only one God, but He is continuously manifesting Himself in different forms, in different religions and through different masters, saints, and prophets. We cannot say that first there was no God and then, suddenly, there was God."

We rounded the corner and entered the long street that runs straight to the tomb of Mevlana. Long lines of people waited outside the museum in front of the mosque and vendors plied a busy trade selling curios, plastic prayer beads, scarves, prayer hats, and small phials of perfume. Flocks of pigeons wheeled and circled overhead.

In the courtyard of the tomb, a rose garden filled the air with scent and the continuous sound of running water could be heard from a large fountain built for people to wash before entering the building to pray. I walked behind him through the museum until we came to the place where the body of Mevlana lies under a heavy cloth of green and gold embroidery that covers the raised bier. We stayed for a long time, and I recall asking not only to be healed of my ignorance but also to know the question arising at the moment, which, if answered, might bring us *all* closer to the truth.

We walked quietly through the different rooms, looking at the illuminated manuscripts and paying our respects to those men of God who rested there.

I sensed a change in myself since my last visit. Then, I had felt an unlimited time for things to work out in whatever way that they should, but now I had the very distinct sensation that time was short. Whether this feeling arose from my own projections, or whether there were other forces at work, I could not tell.

We sat in the courtyard after we came out of the museum, and when the time seemed right I spoke about my feelings.

"Do you find this a problem?" he asked. "Do you remember how many times I have told you that really there *are* no problems? You get so caught up in the world of time that you cannot begin to come to understand the real world. Of course, things change and, indeed, are changing. But how should that be a problem? The only problem that exists is our own ignorance, for it is we who make life so difficult. I dislike this word *problem* in the English language. It is just a concept of the mind that is limiting, and I am sure you did not come back to meet us only to recreate illusion.

"What you call a "problem" is merely an unattended situation. It is quite clear. You have come all the way from England, but you do not know what to ask. Thus, all we can do together is to talk and enjoy being with each other,

13

for destiny can only work to the extent that we put ourselves in its stream, and that, again, has to do with the quality of our intention.

"The most important thing to understand at this juncture is that it is we who have to change. We cannot expect change of others without making efforts of our own. We would only see more and more so-called problems in the outer world. When we cannot solve these problems, we may feel impotent and frustrated, and that will most likely lead us to grief and fear. Before we know where we are, we have either become fanatics, or else we have retired further and further into ourselves and our relationships to escape the pain. Do you see what I am getting at? It is only by changing ourselves that we can see through what we call a "problem" into what underlies it. The unattended situation is within ourselves.

"We have to look at what motivates us, at our repeated habit patterns, and at why we react as we do. If we are honest with ourselves, a change can occur, and we can hopefully see through the illusion of the problem.

"So," he said, "is your mind still full of confusion? What keeps you from asking a real question? Really, all you have to do is to ask for what it is that you lack in your understanding, for what would enable you to be of more service. Or should I break an egg on your head?" He laughed.

I was finding myself more and more agitated. Of course I wanted to know the question, but it had never occurred to me that the majority of the so-called questions I had asked before were merely spontaneous pleadings. They were not really based on experience and study. Now, after years of training, I could, as it were, *feel* the question within me, but for the life of me I could not get it into the right words. The frustration was intense. It was a sense of pain, a yearning to know something that could change my life and perhaps the lives of those around me. I felt irritated with myself. Why couldn't I find the words to express the longing?

We sat out in the courtyard. A steady stream of people was entering the museum. The call to prayer had just begun from the mosque in the square.

I found myself getting muddled, but he read my thoughts. "Finding the answer is not so complicated but finding the exact question can be a subtle and difficult process. One word placed in one part of a sentence may produce an answer that in another part of the sentence will produce something entirely different. We have to learn to be so accurate with our questions that the answer is as clear and simple as possible. Just try to remember that thought, like life, is not linear but cyclical. Everything is turning back to its source. After all, is not Sufism called "the Path of Return?"

"What is it that you truly need just now? What would you most like to know?" There was silence for a while.

It came to me quite clearly, as though a window had been opened in front

14

of me. I could see that there was something badly missing in my life. I had noticed it before, but the pain of seeing it had always meant that I would put the question to the back of my mind. I also found that I was in the grips of a very deep fear; the fear of saying the wrong thing, of making a mistake, of failing some cause that lies beyond the run of everyday life.

I felt like a child. The sweat ran down my face. I could not look up. I could only trust, with all of my being that very shortly something would happen to break the intensity. I simply could not go on like this and it was perfectly obvious that he was just going to sit there smoking cigarette after cigarette.

What is it that a child needs? What is it that brings security to the child?

As the realization dawned on me that I could actually see, I found myself struggling for air. My teacher noticed it. "Keep going," he said. "You are close to the answer. Remember, I asked what it was you *needed* most. I know that you are ready to receive the answer within and thus be able to ask the question. Just let it come."

It was so clear. "I need to know I am loved."

"Good," he said gently. "Now we can proceed."

3

We left the museum courtyard in silence. How could I speak of the realization I had just had? It would sound almost too banal, too naïve, just to say that what would perhaps change the whole course of my life would be to know that I was loved. I knew that my teacher understood, that he was kind, and there was no need to speak at that moment.

Outside the museum, he turned to me and said that we had been invited to attend a special gathering that evening. "You are welcome to come," he said. "These people are my friends. They are "Brothers on the Way." I will be around at eight o'clock to take you if you wish." With that, he excused himself, and I watched him walk on up the street.

The evening meeting turned out to be a late night session as so often happened in Turkey. Anticipating this, I had rested in my hotel room for the few hours that remained before the agreed time. It had been a day I would never forget: there was so much to digest that I was sorely tempted to stay in my room, but I had not come all the way to Turkey to be alone. I was here to discover what direction my life would take. What was more, I had been unable as yet to really speak about the realization I had come to and I knew I must do so sooner or later.

I can't be certain, but I believe the house we visited that night was the same one I had been to some years before. Certainly I recognized many of the faces from previous visits, and there were the usual greetings while cups of tea were brought in from the kitchen. Shoes were piled high by the door and when I got used to the low lighting I realized how many people there were in the room.

Our host showed us to an empty space, and very soon a group of musicians started to play. Everyone present made two circles, kneeling on the ground with their arms tightly interlocked. I was in a dervish gathering once again.

I joined with them in "Dhiqr"—the sacred practice of the remembrance of God. Three drummers and two flute players wove an intricate pattern of music; at the same time, one man sang from the Koran in Arabic, while we chanted the name of God in unison, the music always in our hearts. One by one, the dervishes got up, went to the centre of the floor, and started turning, whirling and whirling, faster and faster, recalling the vortex of life itself.

The Dhiqr lasted well into the night. At the end of the evening, an old sheikh who had been very kind to me on previous occasions came forward. He had had great influence on my life, and I always had felt myself cleansed in his presence. "Ah," he said, embracing me deeply. "It is good to see you once more in Konya."

Much later, my teacher and I walked back to the hotel, agreeing to meet for breakfast the next day. He said that he wanted to explain certain things and also to see whether I had understood anything during the day. I suspected, when I saw the glint in his eyes, that he sensed what I had experienced but still did not know how to express. That night I lay awake, watching the early light creeping up over the roofs of Konya and hearing the dawn call to prayer from the minarets throughout the city.

"So," he said, as the breakfast was brought to us. "Where do we go from here?" The question took me aback, since I had fully expected the answer to be provided for me. As so often, I had been caught by my own presumptions. My teacher was a master of this, always setting me up so that I would have to fall back on what lay within.

"I want you to go back to the question," he continued. "You may have had some sort of helpful realization, but if you are not quite clear about what you have understood, then little good will come of it. As I have said, more people do not prepare themselves to ask questions.

"It is like the art of conversation. Real conversation," and here he leaned forward to make his point clear, "real conversation arises when two or more people agree to come together in the name of a question. Each person offers a contribution, adding to the distillation. What is left, however, is not an answer, but a deeper question. On her deathbed, Gertrude Stein was approached by a great friend and confidant, who asked her, "Well, Gertrude, now for the answer." "No!" said Gertrude, with her last breath, "Now for the question."

He continued, "You have come all this way to Turkey to ask for my advice. Now it is essential that you express in words what you must perceive. It is not enough just to think you know the question. It is necessary both to ask it in words and perhaps even to write it down, so that you are quite certain you know what you want. Now, tell me, did you not receive some sort of understanding after I left you in the museum?" He smiled. "Don't worry, if you took all the trouble to come to see me in Turkey, it was also up to me to take the trouble to do all that I could to find out what you really wanted and then to help bring it out into the open."

Taking a deep breath, I turned round to face him, "If I knew that I was loved," I said, "would I not begin to know the source of love itself?"

He smiled again and nodded his head in acknowledgement.

We talked on into the day. I was made to face this question from every angle. I had thought that I was quite clear about what I was asking, but the more that we analyzed it, the more complex and fascinating it became. We touched on psychology, on Freud and Jung, and how they would have approached the situation. We discussed the implications of what, perhaps, knowing the answer would bring forth from within. I was asked to reach deeper and deeper into the question until he was perfectly satisfied that we could go no further at that time. Finally he turned to me and said, "There is a punch line that could be useful. If you know that you are loved, and thus come to the source of love, what is the effect? What is the meaning of the famous saying in our tradition, "Love is the cause, and Love is its own effect?"

"But enough! This afternoon and this evening I am busy, but tomorrow we can go to Ephesus to visit the Chapel of the Virgin Mary. We will go and pray that you will be guided on your way, for I sense that it is time for a great change in your life. To be quite sure, we need to ask."

The next morning we set off early on the bus for the long journey to the port of Izmir. There we would hire a car to take us to Ephesus. It was a good day, and much of the tension that had been building for so long had gone. I felt as though I was once more connected to the Way, and the experiences of the past two years were beginning to fit into place. It was even possible to realize how each one of these experiences had, step by step, led me to understand what I needed, and how that understanding was so necessary to be passed on to others.

I had been to Ephesus before and looked forward to it. There is something very special about the place. Since my first visit, I had sensed that the Virgin Mary held a meaning that I had yet to understand. We talked much about this on the bus. He told me that Mary is held in esteem by Christians and Moslems alike and that, since there is an inner, esoteric understanding that underlies all religions, this was not mere coincidence. He also reminded me that in every mosque in the world the *Mihrab*, or prayer niche in the eastern wall of the mosque, is dedicated to the Virgin. "It's a pity more Christians do not know this," he said laughing. "Mary is the perfect woman, complete in herself, having the perfect matrix, the perfect receptacle from which Jesus could be born."

We stayed in a small hotel just by the fish market in Izmir. That night we ate fish straight from the sea chosen by ourselves from the baskets that lined the roadway outside the market. I sensed that it would not be long before I would make another journey, but nothing was spoken about it that evening, and we retired to bed early, tired after the long bus ride.

We drove the hired car to Ephesus the next morning and my teacher suggested that we climb the six kilometers to the chapel on foot as thousands of pilgrims do each year. Once before, I had made the pilgrimage in December, and the freezing winds had made the walk anything but pleasant. This time it was another matter. Birds were singing; the hills were covered in wildflowers, blankets of blue and yellow gently moving in the breeze, and the air was filled with the smells of spring. We waved greetings to the shepherds who were leading their goats out to pasture, and our steps seemed to get lighter and lighter as we reached the top of the hill. We looked over the plains and meditated on what it must have been like, nearly 2,000 years ago, when Mary first came here after the death of her son. We bought candles outside the chapel and, lighting them in prayer, placed them in boxes of sand sparkling with other candles left by those who had already visited earlier that day. A nun was kneeling in the front, and I watched the intensity of her prayer. In the pew behind, three Moslems, equally deep in prayer, stood with their hands open and raised in front of them. My eyes filled with tears. Somehow I knew that my own prayers were already answered.

That night, my teacher turned to me and said what came as no surprise, "It is time for you to leave and go back to England. Destiny brought us together once again, but this time you found the answer without being told. It is a good sign, and I shall pray that you will continue to be guided along the path that you have chosen. There are one or two things that I would like to say to you. So please listen, for words have difficulty expressing such things.

"I once said to you that the answer lies in the egg. That was to get you interested enough to ask for the real meaning behind my words. If you had not been interested in healing and the spiritual arts, I might have put it in another way; but if you now relate the egg to the matrix and remember what I have said about Mary and Jesus, you may understand on a much deeper level. Never take things on their face value alone. There is always something else that underlies whatever you see or feel. Do you remember what I said to you those years ago, "Your body is the Virgin Mary; the spirit is Christ?" The mind cannot understand these things, but there is another, inner sense that can comprehend. If you always remember that there is one God, one absolute being, which is the principle underlying all religion and all true paths, then, little by little, these inner senses will develop usefully.

"You want to know that you are loved. 'God loves you,' it is said, but there

20

is only God. Think about this, for there must be no more duality in your life. The key for you is woman in her many aspects. That is why I took you to Ephesus. Can you understand?

"Everything you see here in the relative world is what we call a "witness" of God. It is the form that may carry the essence, but by itself it is no more than a shell. Thus, when I say it is time for you to study woman in her many aspects, I mean the deeper and deeper levels that can be understood. If you will remember that there is only one God, then His manifestations will be seen to be the expressions of His Love. Turn to the highest and know that you will be looked after, as you are indeed loved. May God grant you freedom."

We sat silently, and then he went upstairs to bed. Although what he had said was not really a surprise, there was once more that feeling of sadness and separation that I had had the last time that I left Turkey. It was different this time, though, for I could see that life really is the teacher, and so those that help us on the way are manifestations of life, which is God's gift to us.

Just to remember to always be grateful! I walked along the road by the hotel meditating on this. A half moon hung over the ocean. The sky was filled with stars and seemed to go on forever. Fishing boats were in the bay. You could just see their outlines in the moonlight, their lamps sending out shimmering lines of light towards the shore. It was not hard to be grateful that night.

When I got back to my room, there was a note on my bed. "Dear Friend," it read, "Here is the name and address of a woman in London. I have known of her for many years and you can trust her implicitly. Go to her soon. In the meantime, I will write her a letter by way of introduction, explaining some of the things that have transpired between us over the years. She will lead you on the next step of your journey. Again, I remind you not to take things at their face value.

"I am going to leave very early in the morning, so if I do not see you, don't worry. I have to go back to Konya for a while, but I will make prayers for you each day at the Seat of Mevlana."

The letter was signed in Arabic. I put it beside my bed and was soon asleep. For some reason, I did not wake up until late the next morning. The man behind the desk told me, "Your friend has gone, and he has paid the bill for you both."

4

My flat in London was on a busy street, but the sitting room at the back of the house was quiet and looked out over a beautiful garden. I had arranged the furniture so that I could sit by the window, and I often watched the changing scene for hours. The regulars became familiar, children playing, people walking their dogs and a serious group of men who flew their kites at ten o'clock on Sunday mornings. A tiny lady came by every now and again with all her belongings in plastic bags piled high on a battered children's pram. Every time I returned from a journey, I spent some time by that window re-establishing where I was, getting ready to pick up the pieces and proceed with my so-called normal life.

On this particular occasion, the contrast was even more marked than before. London was a far cry indeed from the Anatolian plains, whirling dervishes and esoteric meetings. I felt quite clear that this was the last journey I would make to Turkey, for in England lay the answer to my question.

I had arranged to be in the Middle East for a long time, and so I had returned with no plans except to visit this woman called Elizabeth. For a while, time was on my side.

I decided not to see anyone for three days, nor to call any of my friends. It was a necessary period of preparation; I had learned over the years not to take lightly the instructions I had been given. I wanted to be prepared and ready to accept whatever would happen.

I rested, followed the spiritual practices I had been taught, and contemplated deeply what I had been told about woman and the matrix of life. More and more it became clear that there was an inner meaning in the recognition of woman exactly as she is that I had yet to understand. The word *recognition* conjured up many ideas; and I was intrigued to discover that it literally means "to know again that which is already there."

I remembered meeting a young woman in southern Turkey several years before. She had screamed one evening in a way that I now realized was a cry for recognition. She was considered mad, as she was obsessed with a ball of blue wool, that she carried constantly, searching for its end, but my teacher had understood that there was a strong chance he could help her to know she was recognized—at least by one person. The last time I saw her, I was amazed at the change in her and at how the shattered pieces of her mind had come together. Order had somehow appeared out of the chaos of her despair.

Woman, mother, Mary, matrix, earth—perhaps Elizabeth, the woman I was going to visit, would be able to tell me more about these things. I remember feeling excited as I drove to the south of London where she lived. I did my best not to expect anything, but when I telephoned her to make an appointment she already knew that I was coming. "Ah yes," she said to me rather briskly. "You're the man who has just come from Turkey. I know your teacher. We have some mutual contacts and friends. Of course you can come. Would you like to have lunch with me on Thursday?"

Elizabeth was definitely not what I had expected, and it amazed me to recognize how I kept falling into the trap of imagining how people ought to be. I was sure that she would be living in a small house with a lovely garden in which she grew roses and sweet smelling herbs. In fact, there was no garden to speak of. The house was a late Victorian, semidetached, and rather dark and gloomy from the outside. She was wearing a Scottish tweed suit with her hair brushed firmly back into a tight bun at the back of her head. She was small in size, rather stocky, and, due to the way the tweed suit was cut, appeared almost entirely square in shape. To complete the image, she had a monocle on a piece of black string around her neck.

"Do come in," Elizabeth began. "You found the way all right, I suppose, for you're in good time. If you like, we will take sherry before lunch. I'm very partial to a glass myself at this time of day." I had barely had time to stutter a greeting and follow obediently as she showed me into the little sitting room and then disappeared toward the kitchen. I had a few moments to look around. I think I must have expected the walls to be lined with esoteric books and manuscripts, because I was somewhat let down by the spotlessly clean and well-dusted room, which gave the impression that it had remained exactly the same since Victorian times. The small desk against the wall was neatly stacked with writing paper and a file for unanswered letters. A box of matches and sealing wax rested side by side on a rose-patterned dish. On top of the desk was a collection of family photographs in oval silver frames, while above hung a large pastel portrait of a young girl whom I guessed to be Elizabeth. The chair seats were covered in petit point depicting mixed baskets of garden flowers, and a tall glass case held an interesting collection of china and Waterford glass. Beside Elizabeth's chair was a small table on which lay a Bible. I was just about to see which edition she had when she returned with a silver tray, two glasses, and a crystal decanter of sherry.

"Now then," she said, putting the monocle into her right eye and pouring sherry into the glasses. "I'm getting quite blind in one eye, so I've got to wear this ridiculous eyeglass. I can't stand spectacles. I lose them, or they fall off my nose. And anyway, as only one eye is bad, I only need one piece of glass, don't I?" She laughed then, a sort of bubbling sound that came up from deep in her belly. It was a wonderful laugh, and during the time that I knew her, I heard it many times. She would produce it at critical moments, particularly when the going was a little tough, and it never failed to make me smile.

"Well, my dear man, here's cheers!" We clinked glasses, and she downed hers with one gulp, quickly refilling it from the decanter. "Come along," she said. "There's only a teaspoonful in there. Drink up and let me refill the glass, and then we can sit down and relax for a bit." I did as I was told and sank back into the leather chair opposite.

"So you have been in Turkey again, I see, as though the answer is not under your nose. I spoke to your teacher once about the way you keep running off to the Middle East, but he said that there was nothing he could do as long as that was what you wanted. He simply waited to meet you at the other end. But tell me about yourself."

I went over the events that had brought me to her: how I had gone back to my teacher to seek further direction, and how he had sent me back to England. Finally, I explained my realization about what was missing in my life and, indeed, in most people's lives, the knowledge that we are loved.

"But surely you have learned a bit more than that after all these years," she said laughing. "Good heavens, man, that is where we begin, not finish. However, strangely enough I do know what you are getting at, although I might have put it in slightly different terms. I would have said something like, "To know the meaning of Love" or "the purpose of Love," rather than sounding a bit like a small child wanting attention. But forgive me, I am known to be rather rude and brusque. Most people demand love, because they think they ought to receive it. They don't see that real Love breaks us away from anything that is not Love.

"Well, now, can you tell me why you were sent to me? Surely your teacher is perfectly capable of talking to you about these matters?"

"I sense that he feels I need to work with women teachers for a while," I replied. "He has suggested I explore the nature of female energy and the matrix."

"Absolutely," said Elizabeth. If you're ever going to get married in the true sense of the word," she said, wagging her finger at me, "then you most certainly ought to know about these things. It's no good just taking women for granted. Life can be very difficult that way. What else were you told?"

"He also said that there was much that could still be discovered in England, and it was about time I came to appreciate my own country and the West rather than chasing around the Middle East looking for dervishes."

"Splendid!" said Elizabeth, raising her glass a second time. "I'll drink to that. It's about time you realized that, although travelling is good experience and fun, what you are looking for can eventually be found without leaving your room. You probably know that your teacher has lived in most countries of the world, however, including America. I met him here, and although we only met on a few occasions, we agreed to pass on certain pupils to each other if that seemed indicated. Interestingly enough, I have never become involved with the Middle East and the Islamic religion and culture. My training was in India when I was a young girl, but for the past thirty-five years I have been in this house, not going anywhere very much, especially since my husband died, a little over two years ago."

So far I had not really been able to say much. I longed to ask her exactly what she was involved with and what sort of esoteric training she had had. She must have read my thoughts, for she leaned over and opened a drawer in the table beside her. Taking out a small leather-bound volume, she said, "You are probably wondering about my way. I told you that my initial training was in India. Do not be put off if I tell you that now my way is the way of the contemplative, for there are as many paths to God as there are human beings in the world. It might be yours one day; but now it seems you have other things to do. This little book of themes for contemplation was given to me in London just after World War I. There was a very fine school in the Kensington district, and many people went there. It was run by an extraordinary woman to whom I am eternally grateful. Everything she gave us is written in these aphorisms, and it has been quite enough for me to work on for over forty years, although it is not very glamorous.

"I would like to return to this idea of the matrix that we were speaking about earlier. I received a letter from your teacher in Turkey saying he wanted me to set up the conditions for you to understand as much as possible about these matters. So I will do so. Although the knowledge of the matrix has long been held in the inner esoteric schools, much is now being released. However, much also depends on your inner degree of preparedness and work, for the mind simply cannot comprehend these things. Therefore perhaps you could tell me what you have learned and what practices have brought you here."

I found it harder than I expected to answer. Over the years, there had been many different approaches, and many different methods of meditation and concentration. We talked at length. Finally she agreed that the secret of life lies in the knowledge of breath and that the possibility of understanding lies through and within breath.

Elizabeth continued to cross-examine me, and I found myself getting into deeper and deeper water as I tried to explain various theories I had about breath and the ionosphere and how it was possible to change the rate of negative ions in a room simply through the conscious use of breath. Just then I heard someone cough upstairs. For some reason, it came as a great shock. I couldn't explain this, except that I had thought for some reason that Elizabeth lived alone. As I was to learn later, she never missed anything that went on.

"I have had a lodger since my husband died," she said. "I'm getting too old to keep the house as clean as I would like it, and having someone here is very nice for me. As a matter of fact, I believe you two have met." I detected a very definite gleam in her eye. She was twirling the monocle round and round on its piece of string, and then, to my astonishment, she popped it into her mouth! She watched me for a few moments but I felt I would be intruding to ask her directly. Noticing my hesitation, she relented. "Don't worry yourself about it," she said. "You'll know soon enough, and, anyway, it's time for lunch."

I began to feel that all this had, in some strange way, happened before. The experience of *déjà vu* was almost overwhelming. I felt compelled to mention it to Elizabeth. "How do you explain these things?" I asked her. "The sensation is incredibly strong. It is as though I am walking into a situation that is already set up."

She seemed to take little notice of what I was saying, busying herself at the sideboard. "I have made a cottage pie," she said. "I do hope that it will suit you. Now, why don't you sit down and start," she said, handing me the plate. "I don't like my food to get cold."

The dining room was intimate and furnished in the same style as the sitting room. French windows opened onto a small patio. A pair of budgerigars was chattering noisily in a cage hanging by the window, and I was reminded of the birdcages in Mexico. Elizabeth noticed that my mind was wandering. "Come along now," she said brusquely. "Eat up. I can't have my food spoiled by wishy-washy thinking."

There was polite conversation during the meal, but I sensed that she was waiting until we were finished before saying anything further. This was confirmed when she stood up to get fruit and cheese.

"You know, it is so important to eat consciously. To be involved with the conscious transformation of energies, you must be doubly careful how and what you eat. If you are preparing food, you must be very, very aware." I was reminded of the love with which my teacher had cooked food for his guests.

"Now, then, what about this premonition you have?" she said, changing the subject rapidly. "Does it really matter? After all, if something is to be, if we don't get in the way, then it will be. Isn't that right?"

"I have had such experiences before, Elizabeth, but something feels different this time. I mean, it's pretty strange going all the way to Turkey from England, only to be sent back to meet someone who lives in the same city."

She smiled at me, playing with her monocle once again. "In Turkey, that is called *kismet*, which means destiny. I am sure that you have often heard the word used. It is a good word and describes many things in just two syllables. You see, fate is not destiny, although most people confuse the two. The difference is subtle, but quite clear when you understand. If our ultimate goal is completion in the knowledge of God then we have taken a very real step towards finding our true destiny. If, on the other hand, we do nothing about our own conditioned responses to life and the situations in which we find ourselves, then we are in very great danger of being carried away from our true destination, of being subjected to the vagaries of fate that in a sense, has a life of its own. We must not tempt fate. As the American poet Ralph Waldo Emerson said, "Woe betide a man who has been overcome by fate, the control of which has slipped his hands."

"Destiny, on the other hand, can be likened to a river flowing back towards the ocean and the realization of our unique possibility in God. If we can let ourselves be carried gently by this river toward our true origin, then we will be fulfilling our purpose in being born.

"There are ways to put ourselves within reach of the workings of destiny," she went on. "If, as we say, 'you're on top of it!'—that is, on top of the breath—that is a start. If you are truly in the present moment and not carried away by your thoughts and fantasies, you are also in a position to be free of fate and available to destiny. For example, on the very day you telephoned, I received a letter from your teacher, saying that you were coming. Perhaps that was destiny. Who knows? Either way, you are here, and we will wait and see. Your teacher did say in his letter however, that kismet had brought you to him in the first place and that kismet guided him to send you to see me."

"Well, can I still ask who is upstairs?" I ventured. "Perhaps that will answer everything."

Elizabeth smiled, and again I heard the beginnings of that rumbling cough, turn into her famous laugh. This time it took longer to emerge, but when it did the laughter came out of every bit of her. She leaned back with her hands on the waist of her tweed suit and laughed with complete abandonment. I, too, was soon hooting with laughter so that the china rattled in the cabinet. She wiped her eyes with a handkerchief and then carefully cleaned the monocle before reinserting it into her right eye. "I have been naughty, but you'll get used to it. I just cannot resist. I find life so full of humour. It's a set-up, was all set up at the beginning, but until we understand we still think that we can do something about it. All we can really do is to agree to the set-up and then play the game. Splendid!"

"All right, my friend," she continued, "I will put you out of your misery." Opening the door of the dining room she shouted upstairs. "Nur, come down, I have a friend I want you to meet."

"Now, she doesn't know," Elizabeth went on, "who is here for lunch. I could have told her, but I decided that it wouldn't matter anyway."

I had no idea what to expect. Elizabeth obviously loved the mystery of it all, possibly at my expense, and I think that if it hadn't been for her extraordinary laugh I would have been quite offended. As it was, I found myself happily accepting the play. I heard the sound of someone walking downstairs and a knock on the door.

"Come in! Come in!" Elizabeth said. In through the door walked the girl I had known in Turkey, the girl whose haunting obsession with the ball of blue wool and whose recovery I had never forgotten. Something about her had moved me deeply then, and I had searched fruitlessly for news of her when I had first returned to England.

I cannot remember now the first impressions I had; her beauty, the way she held her body, or the way she seemed to glide across the room to meet me. Her posture was perfect, and the change in her since the first time we met was so striking that I found myself unable to take my eyes from her face. Gone was the tangled hair and mute face. Instead, she was a beautiful woman, perfectly composed, emerging metamorphosed out of her own past. I couldn't help chuckling, however, when I noticed that she had on one foot a red sock, and on the other a blue one. Otherwise she was exquisitely dressed. A pink scarf was wound around her neck, and her hair was long, almost to her waist.

"Give her a kiss or something," Elizabeth said. "Nur, put him out of his misery."

It was obvious that she was as surprised to see me as I was to see her. It had been nearly three years since we had last met and I had watched her leave Turkey with a party of Australians who were driving to England. We held each other in silence for a long while. I noticed the rhythm of her breath. It was the same as my own, the one I had been taught all those years before.

"I imagine you two have a lot to catch up on," Elizabeth said tactfully. "I'm feeling tired now, and I am going upstairs for my afternoon rest. You can stay and talk. And, Nur, you are not, I repeat *not*, to do the dishes. We will all do them later." With that she walked out of the door, the noise of her shoes on the wooden floor a contrast to the almost soundless walk of Nur in her stocking feet.

After Elizabeth had gone, Nur and I were left in a space that was new to both of us. We were not embarrassed. Perhaps we were shy, but then that is ridiculous, since I was now nearly forty-one. We were in the middle of a *déjà vu* experience of our own, let out of time into a different dimension. The world stood still, and yet at the same time we could see it unfold. Stillness and movement, a perfect balance of the two. Time and space were fused for those moments. We did not speak, but I remember taking her hands in mine. We knelt on the floor facing each other. Our heads touched in the silence. Then the telephone rang. Not wanting Elizabeth to waken, I let go of Nur's hands to answer it. The ringing stopped before I reached the phone, but the moment was broken.

We looked at each other for a while, still not saying anything, but the tension became unbearable, and I broke the silence. "*Nur* means 'light,' doesn't it? Where did the name come from?"

"It does mean light," she said. "However, it is better translated as the all-apprehending Light of God. I was given the name after I returned to England."

"So how did you come here? I mean, have you been with Elizabeth all the time since we last met in Turkey?" We were both fumbling for something to say. "This is ridiculous! Where do we start?"

Nur looked at me. She raised my eyes from the state of confusion I was in and took them into hers. For a brief moment, I felt again that sensation beyond form or time.

"Forgive me," she said. "Sometimes I do not talk very much. When you met me, I did not speak at all as I was very fragile and only just recovering from what had happened. Now I find little necessity to speak, so please don't worry if I am silent some of the time. We are going to be travelling together, aren't we?" It was more a statement than a question.

Her forthrightness took me aback. But it *was* clear that we would be together now. We had met in a world unhindered by the conditions of our normal existence and were being carried onward by something greater than ourselves.

"It's not the time to talk about it just now," she went on. "I didn't expect to see you either, but I have learned to go with the tide these days. I don't resist it as I used to, so I find so much joy in being alive." We spoke quietly then, of her journey to England and her meeting with Elizabeth. We lapsed into silence for a time, and then Nur moved over to a very old phonograph in the corner. It was housed in a heavy mahogany cabinet of the type produced just after the war. She put on Vaughan Williams' *Towards the Unknown Region,* and we sat together. All sense of separation vanished. I did not think of her, nor she of me. We allowed ourselves to be carried by the sounds of Vaughan Williams' music. We became one with it as was everything else in the room, vibrating to the sound. As it moved toward the finale, I realized how Walt

Whitman's words had so inspired the composer:

Darest thou now, O soul,
Walk out with me toward the unknown
   Region,
Where neither ground is for the feet
   Nor any path to follow?

No map there, nor guide ...
   All is a blank before us,
All waits undreamed of in that region,
   That inaccessible land.

The moment was so vast that our bodies reverberated and broke with it.
The melting into union, as I had never known it, happened for us both almost
simultaneously. We met in a world beyond attraction and emerged into a
world of pure light. It was a taste of eternity, and it changed our lives. We were
not even holding hands.

5

"Ah, there you are, then," said Elizabeth, coming down the stairs. "It must be about time for tea." I noticed an old grandfather clock in the corner that was whirring but did not seem to want to strike. "That clock drives me mad," she went on, "always trying to strike the hour but only occasionally making it." She walked over to the corner and slapped the side of the case. After a chorus of sounds, the clock struck eleven times, which made no sense, because it was four o'clock. The contrast to the power Nur and I had both been experiencing made us burst out laughing.

Elizabeth smiled. "Well, it's been several years since you last met. Have you told him all your life story yet, Nur?"

"I'll get the tea," Nur demurred, smiling, already moving out of the room in that effortless manner I first noticed.

"Good," said Elizabeth. "The chocolate cakes I am so fond of are in the big round tin on the shelf. You could bring those as well. We shall have tea in the proper English manner. You can keep your Turkish coffee!" Again there was a deep rumbling that presaged one of her laughs. However, this time she stopped it on the way and leaned toward me.

"Nur is an exceptional woman," she began. "I know I don't really have to tell you that, but there are one or two things that perhaps I should fill in. Her yearning to know the truth has always been great, ever since she was a child. I knew her parents, although they have both passed on now and that is why she was sent to me. I have acted as a guardian to her during the period she needed to recover from her illness.

"When she first came, she was mending, but was still very confused as to the real cause of her breakdown. Part of her could remember the journey that she set out on before all this happened, but part of her had forgotten, or should we say had "blocked," some of the keys she needed for her freedom. On the surface, she was suffering from a mental breakdown, which had been partly instigated by bad meditation training. It is frightening how much of that there is around. How dare people take others into worlds they are not ready for?" She clarified her point by waving her monocle at me, like a warning finger.

"What was damaged in Nur was the matrix, a part of the framework from which we are continuously becoming in this relative world. All of our being is continuously being formed, either by higher or subtler intelligences or vibratory worlds in conjunction with the lower world of the elements, or as is more often seen, almost exclusively by our lower or animal natures. Everything that you see, feel, touch, taste, or smell can be said to be the result of the formative, more subtle worlds. That's why it is so often said that this world is a world of illusion. I know that your teacher has spoken to you of these things, but in the main I feel it is best not to talk much about it, unless at the right time, with the right person, and in the right place. Otherwise, nothing creative comes out of such conversation."

Once more she smiled and I could see that she knew a great deal more than she was prepared to say just then.

"What I want you to understand, more than anything else, is that Nur has truly been transformed by the death of her own illusions. The trouble is that, even if she has some taste of what this means, it will take someone else to truly recognize her as woman, for what she is in completion. The results of her realization can then be brought into the relative world. You have a special part to play in this. Give her all the space that she needs. Take it from me, and from your former teacher, that she really does know. She does not need to be told anything more, really. Just be with her in breath, as perfectly 'normal' human beings—that is enough. You both will be led by destiny. I am sure of it, so there is no need to force the pace."

I heard the sound of teacups rattling as Nur brought the tray in. The apron she had put on had a large picture of the Queen on the front, which seemed thoroughly incongruous and quite conscious on her part. She carried a beautifully polished silver tray and teapot covered in a humorous, old-fashioned tea cozy. Everything was neatly laid out. The cakes were piled on a silver salver; when most of them had been eaten, I noticed that the salver was a prize given to Elizabeth for horse riding in the 1930s. It made me smile once again to have my conception of a spiritual guide confront this typical, middle-aged English-woman, whose heritage in this land probably went back for centuries.

"Splendid!" said Elizabeth. "Nothing like a good cup of tea. Heaven knows what the English would do without it, and somehow or other it always seems to be there at the right time."

Nur spoke very little during the conversation, but I remembered what she had said. Elizabeth had instructed me to give her all the space I could, so,

34

although I longed to ask Nur many things, the conversation was mainly between Elizabeth and myself.

"Now, from what you have told me of your past experiences, your intention was to find some sort of dervish sect in the Middle East who knew all about healing. But your teacher realized you were not ready for these things and, instead of filling you up with all sorts of information, he prepared some groundwork for you. A play was enacted in which you took part, and the experiences themselves became the teacher.

"Now then," she said, "I would like to set out a program for you since both of you have time to spare. Time is not, however, to be wasted, for waste is the greatest sin. I can get on quite well without Nur being here. The neighbours will come in once in a while, and as long as you both keep in touch that is all that matters. I am to be a spiritual tour guide for you. But, if there is a tour to be taken, then we must discover the aim. It would be stupid if you ran around the world with no aim in mind.

"What we don't want to have is an aim that is vague. Accuracy in all things," she said, slapping her thigh vehemently. Thank God I had a disciplined upbringing. I was simply not allowed to be vague. I had a wonderful mother who taught us to make a decision, meditate on it, ask ourselves whether we were truly willing to do whatever it was, and then to do it, having visualized exactly how and what we were going to do before starting.

"So, let's have a look at why you are here now, and therefore what the real aim and purpose of it all is. What do you yourself think?"

"Well, there is the realization I had in Turkey—and of course there is the whole question about woman and the matrix." I found it hard to express a definite aim. I asked Elizabeth if she would help.

"Tut! Tut!" she commented. "How serious you are. Where's your sense of humour? If you look as serious as that, you'll have no fun at all. That is all I would want for you or for anyone in the world, to live a joyful life and be proud, and that means to be humble, to be alive. Too many people are chasing God, the truth, or whatever, as though it is the end of the world. So let's have a good look at the situation. In the tradition you follow, it is said 'Look to the signs,' is it not? So if we have a peep at the signs, maybe something will come of it. Oh lawks! Wait a bit, it's time for the six o'clock news. I wouldn't miss it. I like to keep up and, anyways, I rather like the announcer's voice." She switched on the radio and leaned back in her chair.

I was completely nonplussed by her action. What could be so important about the news at that moment? It was true, the announcer's voice was very pleasant, but, as far as I remember, nothing new was being reported. There was the usual trouble in the Middle East; a murder in central London; three or four strikes; and the Queen had gone to Scotland to open a new building.

35

Elizabeth, however, seemed to thoroughly enjoy it all and she only turned off the radio when the sports report came on.

"There," she said. "Now what were we saying? Oh yes, I remember, it's about what you are going to do in this next period."

I noticed that my agitation and heaviness had gone. Perhaps my mind had been taken from it by listening to the news, but I did feel strangely lighter.

"Sometimes it is good to stop and listen to something else," she said with a twinkle. "It provides time for work to go on at another level.

"I am going to send you to a very special friend of mine who holds knowledge of what you really want to know. I realize that it is not possible to verbalize the purpose of the journey exactly, since there are always hazards, and things can change. However, in order to understand what this person can give you, it is necessary that we look, once again, at what can separate us from knowing about the real world.

"We say that there are three walls that divide us," she went on, shifting into a serious vein. "These are the walls of envy, resentment, and pride. If we look carefully at our own degrees of these three negatives, we can see what motivates us, and also what blocks us from hearing and seeing the truth. Listen carefully now and you will have something to work on each time you find things difficult to explain.

"The first wall, envy, is much more subtle than we normally think. Of course, envy produces greed, avarice, and such things, but has it occurred to you that it is through envy that we try to have someone else's experience? By now you surely know that this is a ridiculous attempt, since no two moments are alike. The experience that one person has can never be the same as another's. Envy makes us strive after something that is not our own, that is not real, and so what we think we feel is only a watered down version of someone else's reality. So do not, under any circumstances try to copy someone else. You must have something real for yourself, and then you have something real to give another."

She turned to Nur. "Do you remember, dear," she said. "How I explained to you that one of the reasons you got yourself into such trouble was that you went searching for someone who could create in you an experience of what you called 'reality?' Because there was no one around to explain these matters to you, you landed up with quite the wrong person. But perhaps it wasn't as bad as all that," she said, smiling gently. "After all, now you are mended and reformed in another way, and that's better than repeating the same mistakes again."

Nur looked at me and rested her hand on my arm. "Elizabeth is right," she said. "I did not know better then. I understand now that there will always be distances in our togetherness for true relationship to be possible."

"Now the second wall, the wall of resentment," Elizabeth continued, "can be seen all over the place, can't it? Look at how much we resent others or the situations in which we find ourselves. Are we not always trying to change something that is just what it is? And when we find that we cannot, we resent it. It is a beastly disease; quite as bad as the chicken pox I had when I was nearly forty. I was covered with sores, and I wouldn't wish that on anyone!

"Resentment comes from trying to change something we have no right to change, and this, like the other walls, is caused by shock that we have had in our lives."

I remembered when I was fifteen and a half years old; my mother had remarried and taken us away from the beautiful house in which I had been brought up. It was there that, even as a child, I experienced what it meant to see through the looking glass into the real world. When I was eight, I became deeply fascinated by the world of nature, and our gamekeeper became my first teacher. Whenever possible I went out with him into the woods and forest while he made his rounds of the five-hundred acres we owned, watching for poachers and vermin who might attack the game. It was during the Second World War, and food was so scarce that we relied extensively on what we could find in the wilds, most particularly rabbits.

Mr. Taylor was an extraordinary man, a mystic in his own right and although only partly educated, he was able to transmit an enormous amount about the world of nature that he knew and loved so well. For him the realization that everything in life is interconnected was easy. He spent long hours showing me how rabbits in the same field would respond immediately if one rabbit was disturbed, and that by stamping its back legs in warning all the rest of the animals and birds in the area would instantly be on the alert through the vibration set up at that moment. Sometimes, he took me out at dawn to sit by a particular gate and watch the change from night into day, seeing the night creatures return to the forest and the birds wake up in song.

I was just ten years old then. Taylor taught me well in the two years I went with him. I learned to carry a gun and to shoot accurately. I knew all the rabbit holes and hiding places on the estate and I knew how to make the sound of a rabbit thumping the alarm and how to judge the way it would run from its 'seat' if it had to. I learned to love the land and its creatures so deeply that they became a part of me.

And then the test came. Taylor took me out into the woods. It was a cold winter day, with a little snow on the ground, the sun warm and bright overhead. He did not say anything, but we had become so close that most of the time words were unnecessary. Very carefully he led me through the paths, then, off the beaten track along the hedgerow by the side of a ploughed field. We walked silently in that space of deep inner silence and awareness that I had practiced for so long. Not a twig cracked under our feet.

It was not very long before he held out his hand, signalling me to stop. He pointed down to a patch of dried bracken, lightly covered with snow. It was about six feet away and to the average person would have looked no more than a mound in the snow. There were no footprints, but fresh snow had fallen during the night so the rabbit could have been there before it started.

He signalled me to get closer. Very carefully I approached the bracken, scarcely breathing, every muscle alert. He nodded to me. Now it was up to me to know which way the rabbit was facing. The knowledge and instinct that had developed during those years told me that if I stamped in front of the rabbit it would be impossible to catch it. It was necessary to make the sound of the alarm just behind it and throw myself down onto the spot from which he would emerge.

I guessed correctly, for as I made the noise, the rabbit bolted out of the seat in a flurry of snow, and I fell on top of it, one hand holding its back legs and the other its neck. Taylor nodded again, and in the precise moment that the rabbit died there was such an intensity of love and respect for its life that I was completely opened up to another world. Every tree had an invisible counterpart, every bush the same, and everywhere I looked there was a world of shimmering light. I do not know how long I just stood there, the body of the dead rabbit in my hands, but the memory remained with me all my young life. From that time until my mother sold the house and land when I was fifteen and a half, I could see this matrix of light. It was like a living blueprint or negative of a photograph from which everything in this world was taking its shape and pattern. But the moment we went down the driveway of that land for the last time, I experienced such resentment that the window that had been opened for me, closed once again. I could not see into that other world and I was left with just the pale static replica of that vibrant and subtle matrix that had once been so real for me.

For years I worked on the resentment, but it was only during the time in Turkey that it finally went. At last there was no bitterness. Time, which had stopped at that moment I went down the driveway back to school, flowed on into the present moment, and I could see into the real world again.

"Pride," I heard Elizabeth emphasize pointedly as I quickly tried to refocus my attention, "has to do with feeling that we are special in some way, and that stems from ignorance. The root cause is also from shock, however, and the result of this is that we try to defend ourselves and become arrogant. No one— I repeat, no one—is more special than another, or let us say that we are all equally special." I felt that she was addressing me, however subtly.

"But enough," Elizabeth said abruptly. "Just remember both of you that each moment in essence contains the formative world of all our lives. But this is only available to us when we are truly present. It is up to you to meditate on these things. Nur can help in this since what she thought everything to be, based on her own illusions, has gone, and there is something real remaining."

Nur smiled. "Thanks to you, and to the others who were there for me when I was going through it all." She was talking quietly, and I had to lean forward to hear what she was saying. "I will always be grateful," she said.

"Ha!" said Elizabeth with a triumphant look on her face. "Now that's excellent. Do you hear?" she asked, sticking her monocle firmly in her eye and staring at me intently. "The key to will is gratefulness. I often tell people this, for without will we can do nothing. We are simply splattered all over the place with no real motive or intention. The key to will is gratefulness. If we wake up each morning and are grateful, eat with gratefulness the food that God gives us, and are grateful every moment, that is a start. And since will is necessary for order to prevail, we had better jolly well get on with it!

"Now you two get out and let me go to bed early. Take her out to dinner or something and we'll meet again tomorrow."

She started to get up out of the chair. "Help me up, for heaven's sake!" she said. "Can't you see I'm an old woman now? And anyway, there is something wrong with my knees."

Nur and I took both her arms and gently eased her up onto her feet. "Ugh!" she said. "Fed up with old age, but laughter keeps me going; laughter and experience, but one most certainly produces the other." Her rumbling laugh started as we helped her to the door into the hallway, and as she started to mount the stairs she began laughing in pure joy.

6

Nur and I ate at a bistro in the Soho district of London. I had known the place for over twenty years, in which time the menu had never changed. The owner, Madame Sophie, had cooked and served all those years. It was well known for the quality of its meals and for Sophie, a woman of uncompromising character and compassion.

"I'll be with you in a little bit, darling," she said in her eastern European accent as we sat down. "Got to serve all my customers."

The kitchen was separated from the dining area by a low wall. The staff was under Sophie's guidance, and she employed only those who wished to serve, and to serve well.

"Bring some borscht for my friends, she shouted to the staff in the kitchen. "I make very good borscht, darling," she said to Nur. "And why should you be so lucky finding this one?" she said to me, meaning Nur, before turning to some other customers just entering the restaurant.

Despite Sophie's brusqueness, her warmth made Nur and me feel completely at ease. It was a relief, as I had been nervous and uncomfortable all the way to the restaurant. I had taken Nur to my flat from Elizabeth's so I could wash and change before going out to dinner. But as she had warned, she had hardly spoken. Something needed to grow, and it would obviously take time.

The borscht was wonderful, as promised, and was followed by another specialty of the house, a chicken dish prepared in a white wine and cream sauce. A glass of wine each made the meal perfect, and then Sophie came back to sit with us as the coffee was served.

"So, darling," she began, "where have you been all this time? You don't love Sophie anymore!"

It was true that I had not been to the restaurant for over two years. When I came back to England from the first period in Turkey, I had not wanted to go to places I had frequented before. There had been so many changes in my life, both the outer and inner, that I felt unable to see many of the people that

41

I had known.

"Come now," she went on. "What have you been doing, where have you been, and who's this lovely lady?"

I muddled through an attempt to explain what had transpired but Sophie listened attentively.

"So," she said, "you encountered the Way. I wondered if it would ever happen. You were always so impatient that you pushed it away. Silly man!" she scolded smiling. "After all, I must have known you for very nearly the twenty years that this restaurant has been open, and in spite of all the hints and stories you never seemed to understand.

"Me, I'm a very good fisherman!" she said, taking Nur's hand, "but some fish don't bite—they think they are too important."

"You're much more important than him," she said to Nur. "What is your name, darling?"

Nur replied and went on to explain something of her own life story.

"I don't know what you have done to deserve this one," she said to me, pouring my coffee. "You got a big woman here, darling. You be nice to her and treat her well. She knows much more than you do, so you had better be sensible this time.

"Now then," she said. "Let Sophie give you a little advice: until you know what you are doing when you do what we call 'The Work,' just do the work. If not, then eat well, sleep well, and make love well. Me, I work all the time but still I eat well, and sleep all night—but, darling, no more.

"Listen to Sophie for a moment? Sophie had some people in last night. Nice people, darling, but not very sensible. Sophie told them a story, but they didn't listen.

"They were not here, not in their bodies at all. What a funny thing! Imagine being here in this beautiful world and not inhabiting the body. Think, think, that is all these people do, they are not in their bodies at all, but in their minds. No good that, darling.

"Nur, scold him. I love this man. He's my friend, but you better keep him awake, or he might forget you," she said, putting her arm around Nur and giving her a huge hug. "Then Sophie get cross. Sophie's a big lady. This man's not strong enough to stand up to me. So you scold him all the time. Make him listen."

Nur smiled, and I saw that, at the same time, there were tears in her eyes. She leaned over and put her arms around Sophie's neck. There was silence for a split second and then the door swung open. A raucous party of customers came in.

Sophie turned around toward the door. "What you doing, you noisy lot?" she shouted out. "People don't make noise like that in Sophie's restaurant.

You be quiet and behave. What you think this place is . . . some sort of football game? Come in nice if you want to eat here. Pah! These children. They don't care about food or nothing. Don't care about Sophie, only care about themselves."

I watched amazed as the potential customers became silent, walked out into the street, and re-entered quietly.

Sophie went back to the kitchen then, saying that she hoped to see us again.

That night we stayed at my flat. Together we watched the spring sunlight break out over the streets of London. There was a gentle breeze rustling the leaves of the trees outside in the garden. The air was new and fresh after the rain that had fallen during the night. There was no need to speak, to explain, or even to question what had happened within each of us.

When the sun was well up, we went for a walk in Hyde Park, enjoying the massed beds of yellow daffodils contrasting with the rich green of the grass. We watched the wind moving the flowers. It was a dance with the flowers swaying and curtseying in unison. But we noticed two daffodils, right in the middle of the bed, that had turned against the wind. They seemed angry. Holding her hand, I said to Nur, "Do you see? Perhaps, if we loved these flowers enough in recognition, they would turn round and face the right direction again."

She squeezed my hand in agreement, and we stood quite still for a moment. Nur's hair was blowing behind her. We watched as the two daffodils turned their heads. The sea of yellow flowers was in harmony again.

We went to Elizabeth's late that afternoon. She greeted us warmly at the door of her house and took us into the sitting room. "Well, my dears," she said over the inevitable cup of tea, "you've had a good evening, I'm sure, and I have had time to ponder many things. With the right sensitivity and training, we are sometimes able to attune ourselves to the world of possibilities, although it does not necessarily mean that the things we see will work out quite as we would anticipate. But you've probably heard all this before, I expect.

"I think it fair to say, however, that your meeting with Nur was in the world of possibility. At the same time, it just might not have worked out. You might have deviated from the path for many reasons. Your teacher might not have recognized what was happening, or you might have decided not to take his advice. Equally, Nur could have become bored sitting around here and gone off once again, or I might have been away when you called. Anything could have happened. But it did not, and you met.

"Certain factors helped in this. In the first place, you had met before, and created a very deep impression on each other. Nur spoke to me about it many times, and even once asked whether she should try to get in touch with you. Remember, my dear?" she said, hooting with laughter. Nur smiled. I am not sure that she didn't blush but I could only see half of her face.

"I strongly advised her to keep to herself and wait, for we both wanted to let destiny take its course. You had met; there had been an exchange of energy; there had not been the usual sexual attraction, and thus there were many possibilities. All this damned sexual attraction; people get stuck in it thinking that it is love itself. Rubbish!" she said loudly. "Sex may be an expression of love, but most people land up in bed without considering the meaning of love at all. It keeps the bed manufacturers happy, but love is completely forgotten!

"What was I saying? I'm sorry, but that subject is one of the particular controversies I have with people who come to me for advice, mainly wanting me to agree to their own confusion. Half the psychiatrists' couches and the gurus' ashrams are filled with people like this who do not really want to risk change but who just want the security of feeling better. It keeps the profession going, I suppose, but it doesn't make much real sense. I once heard a definition of a psychiatrist as 'an illusion treating an illusion for an illusionary sickness.' Whoops! I am being naughty now. One day I'm going to get myself into trouble with some of my good friends.

"It so happens," she went on, "that if two people meet on what might be called a spiritual plane and if the time is right, the union of these two souls can manifest in this world. It's no darn good floating around in some angelic sphere having a jolly good time and not doing anything about it *here*. Angels have their own job to do. They haven't got bodies as we do and are thus limited. Now there's a shocker.

"It may also be, however, that two souls meet and it is *not* destined that they are to be together in this world. They touch each other and part. They have other work to do. Yet the meeting can never be forgotten; it is ingrained on the soul itself. Remember, the soul is made up of a special substance that knows itself. It is a 'knowing substance' as the Sufi tradition says.

"In the Koran, there is a saying that 'We will try them until we know,' and although this is not my own background, it does explain something of this process quite well. For, if it is intended that two souls work together, they are tried in this three-dimensional world, although they may actually have met in a world that is not of time and space as we know it—a timeless world to which we are able to return when we have found the Holy Grail within, right here."

44

She thumped her foot on the carpet emphatically, making the teacups jump on the tray. "But there I go again! You have got the whole of your lives to work that one out. No good me telling you all the answers before you have had the chance to have the experience life can give you.

"Let's have another cup of tea and see what's coming up. Nur, dear, please go down and put the kettle on. This tea is so stale now it would tan my innards like shoe leather.

"What is clear," she said as Nur poured the freshly made tea, "is that you need some time together. But, if what I have seen is correct, you must not forget that you are also part of a process that may make you instruments to express something for others to understand. You don't have to *do* anything about it, but you must become conscious of it.

"I think I mentioned yesterday that I wanted you to visit a beloved friend of mine who is living in Wales. I hardly ever see him these days, as I don't have a car, and he is crippled. We write each other, and about once a month we have a long talk on the telephone. Like yourself, he was involved with the dervishes in the Middle East for many years. He has some special knowledge that perhaps he will pass on to you. I shall write to him tonight so if you can spend a few days getting to where he lives he will be ready to see you.

"There are one or two things I need to tell you about him, however," she went on. "The first one is that he is dying of cancer and is in great pain most of the time. No one knows how long he will live, but he is one of the only people I know who is ready to go. He has made peace with his Maker, and that's more than I can say for myself," she said smiling. "I'm still too selfish and enjoy life too much, I expect.

"John's condition is particularly difficult in that he has an open wound on his shoulder and there is sometimes a terrible smell of decay. You must learn not to react to it. Also, since he is paralyzed he is in need of help. There are people who come in every day, but if he invites you to stay for a while, then you must learn from them what is necessary and take over their job for that period.

"Now, is that all understood?" she asked turning to us both, one after the other, to make her point clear. "John could be a spiritual guardian for you both, just as I have acted as godmother to Nur over the last two years. But you must listen, serve, and have much compassion. You will know, then, just how much he loves. And he does love so much, you know, that sometimes I wonder if there is anything else in him."

To my surprise, I heard Elizabeth's rather gruff voice crack a little. "Silly old fool I am," she said, wiping the tears from her eyes. "I love that man so much. We would have married thirty years ago if we could have, but that just was not in the cards. Still," she said, "we must not be ashamed of being

45

human, and I'm as silly as the rest."

As she got up she must have read my own thoughts. I had hardly been around and here I was on my way. "Don't worry," she said, as Nur took her arm, "you'll get used to us one day. So much of life is to do with good timing, isn't it? If you try and fight the tide you always land up in the wrong direction."

"It's time for my rest," she said. "Nur, you go and pack your things. There's an envelope on the dressing table with John's address on it and a map to help you find the spot, as it is very remote. Ring me when you get there. I shall miss you."

She put her arms around Nur, and they embraced silently for a while. "Come here, you idiot," she said to me. "Give your old friend a kiss too." We all three started to laugh. The pressure that had built suddenly melted. I could hear the beginnings of the internal rumble that preceded that extraordinary laugh. "Get on with you," she said, wheezing and spluttering. "You both have a very bad effect on me. Can't seem to stop laughing, and when I'm not laughing, then I'm crying. I'm meant to be a very serious occultist, you know!" She wagged her finger and very deliberately replaced the monocle in her eye. "Ah! That's better. Now no one would recognize me." She smiled, "God bless you both, and may you be guided on every step of your journey."

With that, she turned and went up the stairs. Nur followed her and went to her room to pack.

7

"Let's go to Stonehenge on the way," Nur said. "We could drive overnight and be ready to see the sun come up." After all the tension we found ourselves slightly delirious and happy. It was as though permission had been given and we could go on our way in freedom. We were sitting in the car outside Elizabeth's house. "First we must go back to my flat," I said. "I have to pack a suitcase and leave a forwarding address with the caretaker. We'll have dinner and then we can go."

It was just turning dusk and the street lamps were switched on. People were already returning home. They looked so tired. We both felt sorry and wanted to shout out to them the beauty of life that we felt but I doubt if they would have heard. Perhaps, at that moment, their world was not a world to reason the whys and wherefores of things. Yet it was a world that was just as real for them as our world was for us. What is real for anyone is what one sees with the outer or the inner eye. "We become what we behold," Blake wrote.

I realized that night, that the extraordinary thing about our meeting was the complete lack of reserve we both felt. It was our first dinner together, at least the first time that we had eaten alone, and yet there was such a harmony between us that it was as though the years since we had first met simply did not exist. We shared stories over the Greek meal Nur had prepared. We laughed, listened to music, and were silent. Something about the inevitability of the situation held us continuously. The sensations and feelings were so strong that only the moment existed.

Although I had come from a family background that had been particularly interested in the Druid and Celtic legends, and in the ancient history of the British Isles, I had only been to Stonehenge once before and that was many years earlier to witness a ceremony held by the Druids. Each year they gather together from many parts of England, Scotland and Wales to celebrate the summer solstice within the circle of standing stones. On this one day in the year, the sun breaks over what is called the heelstone and thousands of people come for the event.

I had much preferred the idea of going quietly however, when one could sit alone and ponder the meaning of Stonehenge and of the other stone circles that are found throughout Europe.

Nur and I had driven from London overnight. We had planned the journey to arrive just before sunrise. We were early for it was still dark as we parked the car. The air was chilly, most of the stars had gone and everything was filled with an air of expectancy. You could feel the great mass of the earth turning slowly towards the light of the sun.

Neither of us spoke. As we sensed the first glimmerings of dawn, we walked into the centre of the circle formed by the stones. In the darkness they seemed like great sentinels, their massive shapes standing out against the lightening sky. I was glad to have someone with me and I knew that Nur felt the same way.

It was very close to dawn. A bank of clouds picked up the reflection of the sun before we could see it and the sky turned pink and then red. I took her hand. Quite suddenly it seemed, the sun moved up over the horizon just south of the heelstone. The great monoliths that only a few minutes before had seemed so dark and brooding were now grey and still in the morning light.

I realized then that we were not alone. In the darkness, I had not noticed there were other people standing singly or in small groups around the circle. There was a deep silence. I saw one young man with his arms raised high above his head in salute. A young woman sat in meditation and two older people stood close together in the shadow of one of the stones.

It was as though everyone in some strange way fitted into the harmony of the moment. The realization of the inter-connectedness of all life was so strong that it was as though we were everywhere at once and yet totally awake to the present, the land upon which we stood and the myriad of beings, both visible and invisible, that made up the subtle structure of the Universe. Everything was so quiet. Everything seemed sacred. "You cannot pick a flower without the troubling of a star" wrote a great English mystic.

Nur had her arm around my shoulders. "It's a taste of something very real," she murmured. "Elizabeth used to talk so much about what she called 'the real world,' and how it is only with the inner senses that this can be understood. What we normally see is merely a world of appearances. Our food here is the food of comparison, but in the real world there is no comparison, only continuous creation in each moment from the perfect pattern, or matrix containing infinite possibilities of manifestation. Thus, the shape of the egg contains within itself all of the kingdoms; animal, mineral, vegetable and so on."

"There was a time when I could see all these things but I was not able to express myself." She was talking very quietly. "To the outer world I was mad. They said that I had had a mental breakdown, but actually I never thought it was so. It was just that I couldn't explain what I saw. Do you remember when I couldn't speak much I used to carry that ball of blue wool with me everywhere? The wool represented for me the threads that interlink all life. It was my own ariadne thread and something that I could hold on to, tracing back my own origin and the origin of all creatures. But you do see just how everything is interconnected?"

"I have had a taste of it," I answered. "But I cannot really explain it any better than you could at that time. All I know is that there is something that links us all in a pattern and it is we human beings who stand at each point of the pattern. It is as though these massive stones represent in physical form, a timeless state that exists in each one of us, both anchoring something into the earth and acting as transformers of subtle energies."

The sun had now risen and we sat on one of the fallen stones as everyone else moved away from the circle. The only sound was a lark soaring above the plain. "You know what I think it is all about," Nur said finally. "I believe that these interconnecting lines are not to do with magnetism alone, as some people assume but more to do with electromagnetism. In China they are called "dragon lines" although here they are known as ley lines. By whatever name these lines are known, it is through them that we are subtly connected in this world. The lines are sleeping, dormant, needing to be recognized. It is like woman who also needs to be recognized. But it is through love alone that they come alive, and it is through love that we are able to go beyond the boundaries of personality and greed and sorrow, to enter the world of Reality."

"That is what I think," she said excitedly, "and that is why we are here, you and I. We are here because of the love that has been awakened within us—so that we can experience a little of what it is all about." I felt a strange sense of excitement. Something had changed. Energy took on a new meaning and looking back on that moment, I suppose it could be said that love had awakened a degree of responsibility that I could not immediately face. The worlds of the poem by Kathleen Raine came into my mind:

Because I love
  There is an invisible way across the sky,
  Birds travel that way, the sun and moon
  And all the stars travel that path by night.

Because I love
  There is a river flowing all night long.

49

Because I love
All night the river flows into my sleep,
Ten thousand living things are sleeping in my arms
And sleeping wake, and flowing are at rest.

It began to rain and we walked slowly back to the car to continue our journey. We had no definite plans where to stay, but there were many small hotels and pubs to be found in that area of England. Nur seemed excited. She was in love with everything, including the rain and had opened the window to hold her arm out so that both she and the inside of the car were getting soaked. Despite everything, I found myself getting agitated.

"For heaven's sake, Nur, close the window."

"Why? Don't be so stuffy. You're too serious. You keep chasing after things; they'd come to you, if you'd let them."

"What's that got to do with shutting the window and keeping the car dry?"

"It's got everything to do with it," she said, laughing. "You know by now, don't you, that if you walk in the rain you get less wet than if you run in it? It's all to do with resistance."

"But we are driving in the car, Nur, not walking!" I reached a point of total exasperation and finally stopped near a small wood. I refused to drive on until she shut the window. The situation was ridiculous and embarrassing. Suddenly, almost for no reason, we were in the middle of a stupid row.

"I thought you said that it would be nice to walk in the rain and make love in front of an open fire," she said. "Well, now, here's all the rain, and you won't even have the window open. Come on! Let's go."

"That's ridiculous, Nur. There's no open fire, it's cold, we're right in the middle of nowhere, and anyway, I haven't got a coat."

"What's a coat got to do with it?" She opened the door, pulling my arm.

"You go for a walk if you want to; I'll wait for you here."

"But there's no point in that," she said, shutting the door again. By this time the car was really wet, since the wind had driven the rain in through the open door. Nur sat in the passenger seat and stared out of the window, which was, by now, completely steamed up.

We were at an impasse. "All right," I said. "Let's go for a walk, then. We're both soaked anyway."

I opened the driver's door and started to get out. "It's too late," she said. "If you want to love a woman, you have to learn to be spontaneous. You theorize and theorize, but when it comes to the point you don't move. Why can't you be natural?"

"I am natural, dammit!" I said. "But what the hell's the point of getting wet when there is nowhere to dry off? It's just plain silly."

"You can't get wet," she said, flinging her jersey at me. "See if you can keep dry in this!"

Opening the door, she ran out into the rain. There was a five-barred gate by the side of the road. I watched her slip through it and disappear into the wood. I couldn't see anything from the inside of the car and had to take my handkerchief to clean a portion of the windscreen. That didn't work either, so I opened the side window and shouted after her. There was no answer; just the sound of rain on the car roof and the water dripping off the trees.

I sat there for a while. "Let her get wet," I thought. "I'll wait!"

But it didn't work that way. She did not come back. I waited and waited. Finally, with rain still coming down, I got out of the car, climbed over the gate, and walked up the path through the wood.

But there was no sign of Nur. I looked for an indication that she had come that way, but the path was sodden with water, and there were no tracks. I called, but there was no answer. Finally I saw an opening in the trees. Soaked through and out of breath, I reached the end of the wood. A five-acre field stretched out in front of me. A few sheep were huddled together in the shelter of the trees by the fence. But there was still no sign of Nur.

"Nur!" I shouted, "Nur!"

At that moment, there was the sound of a branch cracking, and leaves hit me on the back of the head. Turning round to ward them off, I saw her.

For a split second, I wondered if she'd gone over the top again. She was standing behind me on the pathway with a long sprig of leaves in her hand. Her hair was hanging down, like rat-tails, her dress almost transparent from the rain. She stood, her feet apart, her eyes laughing, and her back to the path. "Well?" she said.

We found a pub just back from the road, miles from anywhere. We must have looked pretty strange, soaked and carrying one small suitcase as we walked through the door. A young girl greeted us when we rang the bell but she said that she would have to "find her mum" when we asked if there was a room available. We were left in the hall, our wet clothes dripping. Nur had her arm round me. "They were spontaneous in the old days," she said grinning. "They didn't have so much to think about."

The landlady soon appeared from the back of the house. She looked us up and down very slowly, with great suspicion. "So you want a room, then?" she asked, more as a statement than a question. "Would it be for more than one night?"

"It's just for one night. We were on our way to Wales, but we got delayed, and, as you can see we are very wet and muddy. We would really like a room and a hot bath."

She went over to the desk and spent an age checking on the rooms, occasionally looking up to stare at us once again. I guessed that there was no one else staying.

"I have one room left," she said finally. "But dinner is included in the price. You will be wanting supper, won't you?"

When we said we would love to have supper, she seemed relieved and eventually wrote our names down in the register. "Mind your heads," she said, as she led us upstairs. "The beams are very low and people often bump their heads."

She led us to a room at the end of the corridor, turned on the electric fire, and informed us that dinner would be ready at seven o'clock.

The room was well kept. The bathroom next door had an old-fashioned bath on legs that held so much water you could sink right into it with only your face showing. We soaked until we were warm again. Afterward, we slept; I think both of us wanted to be quiet.

I began to feel depressed over dinner. I suppose it was inevitable, really; so much had gone on that it was obvious the pace could not continue. Nur picked up on it very quickly and asked me what was the matter.

"It seems like we've reached the end of a cycle," I said. "Everything has happened so fast, and before we know it we'll be with John. I can't seem to get used to the speed of change. Do you understand?"

"Of course," she replied. "But I have been with Elizabeth long enough not to be surprised at anything. You wouldn't believe what went on in that house in the past three years. She hardly ever went out, but people turned up continuously in the most unlikely circumstances. It was like theatre. First there would be a letter or a telephone call, and then someone would arrive at the front door, out of the blue. What kept me there was my own longing to learn something useful. I feel the same way now, and perhaps if you looked at it that way, you wouldn't be so depressed. Certainly, it is the end of one cycle, but look at it another way—it is also the beginning of another. We're both going to see this man called John, who is dying of cancer. We are going because you were told by your teacher in the beginning that you needed to meet a woman teacher. Well, you did meet one in the form of Elizabeth, and things have been arranged in such a way that we are together, and we are both on our way to Wales. What more do you want?" She laughed, and for a moment the heaviness lifted.

"Tell me more about Elizabeth," I said. "I didn't have much time, and yet both our lives have certainly been altered from the moment we met her."

"No one knows very much," Nur replied. "She has always been a bit of a mystery, even to me, and I suppose that I was closer to her than most. She is so totally self-contained that it is hard to really get to know her. She hinted at certain things, ideas and so on, and left me to work out what she was trying to get at. A small group meets in her sitting room once a week, but she never let me go to it. She explained that the people in the group were specially chosen to do certain work and had met regularly for years. I noticed that they have carried notebooks or tape-recorders, and when they left they never spoke, they just nodded to me as I showed them out of the door. All were about Elizabeth's age, with the exception of two or three younger people. And that's all I know about them.

"What I've felt," Nur went on, "is that Elizabeth is connected, in some strange way, to another group of people whom I have never met. She sometimes gets very excited when she receives certain letters. They come from all over the world, and she spends ages reading them in detail before sitting down at her desk to answer each one. It takes hours. I've learned that it's better not to disturb her when she's writing as she becomes very cross and agitated if she is interrupted. I used that time to visit friends in London or to go to the theatre.

"Which reminds me," she said with a twinkle in her eye, "I had better get in touch with my friends when we get to Wales. They will be wondering what has happened to me, and none of them knows about us yet. I think they'll find it strange after all this time. I haven't been with a man since I first went to Turkey. I was engaged to be married then, but that's another story, and I don't want to get into that now."

"But tell me a bit more about the time you spent with Elizabeth," I said. "Surely you didn't just stay around that house for two years. What did you do with yourself?"

"I told you, I spent time with friends quite often," she said. "And there is so much to do in and around London that it is hard to get bored. Elizabeth had an old car she lent me. There was also the shopping and cooking to get done, the house to be kept clean, visitors to be looked after, and so on. Actually, there is something else that I should tell you. You see, I was sent to Elizabeth after we last met to get myself together. You saw me in several different states in Turkey but it has taken a long time to get stabilized. Elizabeth is a great teacher. I am surprised, in some ways, that she didn't work with you more, but then there will be reasons for that, I am sure, and time will tell. She did give me certain exercises, mainly with breathing and concentration. I spent many hours a week practicing them, and studying different things that she said would help me help others in the long run. So all that took up a lot of time. No, I was never bored; it was not as though I just sat around the house all day long. I'm really grateful for the time I spent with her, and now that that time is over I shall miss her awfully. So you'll just have to stop being depressed and look after me, won't you?"

We talked late into the night. The landlord came in and lit a fire, as the evenings were chilly. He and his wife then retired, showing us where to turn off the lights and explaining that they had to be up early.

Mainly we talked about John. Nur had heard a lot about him, but had never met him herself. She related that Elizabeth had told her it would be necessary to learn a great deal about death and about dying, and that one day there might be an opportunity for Nur to understand how help could be given to those nearing death if someone with knowledge and ability was there for them, to help with the fear that inevitably exists. I had personally experienced death on several occasions, and so this visit to John was not as worrying for me as it was for her.

I was thirteen years old the first time I saw a man die. I was with a group of farmers who were shooting rabbits in a nearby field. One of them got overexcited and shot the man who was standing next to me. I was with him, holding his head until he died. I can never forget the look on his face and the smile he gave me just before he passed.

Long after Nur went to sleep I lay awake thinking about death and wondering just how afraid of it I was, particularly now that I had fallen in love with her. I realized, perhaps for the first time, the truth of all the teachings about the necessity of being aware of death and of not wasting a moment of one's life. More than that, it became obvious how much time I had wasted in useless worry, even in that day. Before going to sleep, I went back over every minute of the day that I could recollect, until, little by little, I was able to rest.

In the morning, we drove on to Wales, stopping only once by the side of a stream to drink the coffee we had brought with us. Nur was very quiet. She had not had time to do her exercises and needed to work preparing herself. She asked me to stop the car just before we drove into the village where John lived. "It's difficult to be totally present," Nur explained. "So I always stop before I go to visit someone. It's a token of respect Elizabeth taught me. She absolutely insisted that I stop for a moment, even before entering her own house from doing the shopping—just so that I was in a thoroughly collected state. You try it!"

8

"Ah, there you are." John had pushed his wheelchair out onto a veranda on the first floor of the house and was looking down at us. "Forgive me for not being downstairs to greet you, but you arrived earlier than I had expected, and it takes me a while to get this contraption and myself down the stairs. But come in, come in—I have been looking forward to meeting you ever since Elizabeth wrote to me."

"Do you want some help?" Nur asked.

"No, my dear," he replied, "I'm used to it. You two go inside, and I'll be with you shortly."

We went into the front hall. My first impression was the incongruity of the furnishings. We were in the heart of Wales, yet the floor was carpeted with a profusion of oriental rugs and two stunning tribal rugs from Anatolia hung on the walls. The furniture was mostly mid-Eastern, inlaid with mother-of-pearl and ivory. Facing the front door was a long walnut table with a sizable collection of photographs. Some were quite old, but they were unmistakably of Konya. I recalled what I had once been told there, by the tomb of Mevlana, "Remember this is your home," and for a moment there in Wales I felt as though I were in two places at once.

We soon heard a bump on the staircase as John carefully manipulated his wheelchair down the last step. We went to greet him and, not knowing what to do, we shook hands rather formally. The lower part of his body was very wasted, but I was impressed with the extraordinary strength of his chest and arms. It was as though the life in the upper section of his body more than compensated for the weakness in his legs.

"Come along, then," he said, pushing himself forward. "This is my special treat to have you here. Let's go and sit in the other room. I'm afraid this one is rather cluttered with bits and pieces of memorabilia but, then, you've recognized some things here, haven't you?"

"Well, it is a bit of a surprise. You'd hardly expect to find all these objects here. I've just come back from Konya, and it makes me wonder quite where I am," I said laughing.

"Well, it is perfectly possible to be in more than one place at a time. It's all done with mirrors, isn't it?"

We followed him into the other room. It was obviously his study. The desk was covered with papers, books lined the shelves, and there was a deep leather armchair by the fire into which he sank, lifting himself up with his huge hands while we held onto the wheelchair.

"Sorry about the mess," he said, "but this is one room no one cleans up. That way I know where everything is. I've a wonderful woman who looks after me—you'll meet her—but even she doesn't come past this door."

"Now, then, there's some whisky in the cupboard over there, glasses and water. We'll get some ice in a minute," he said, pressing a bell by the chair. "We've a lot to talk about. But before we say anything further, I would like to ask you both if you could stay in Wales for an extended period. Would that be all right? Actually, Elizabeth instructed me to ask you so that you could perhaps learn some very specific things. I could never refuse her a request, and it would be a joy to have you here."

"Ah, Fordie," he said as a woman, in her early sixties bustled into the room. "Have you got the ice?"

"Yes, Mr. John, but I'm afraid we have run out of soda water. I'll get some in the morning. I'm ever so sorry."

"Never mind," he replied, "there are many more important things than soda water. I want you to meet my guests. They are invited to stay indefinitely. I shall tell them all about you when you have gone out of the room, and how they are to behave when you're around."

"Mr. John . . ." she replied. I saw that she was blushing.

"You two keep on the right side of Fordie," he said. "She rules this house, and I have to do what I am told these days; but she's put up with me for over eight years in this condition, and I would do anything for her.

"She's a wonderful woman," John went on after she had left and I had poured a whisky out for him. "I couldn't do without her. She does virtually everything in the house. I can't get out shopping any more, and I can't cook, so she's a godsend to me. Her real name is Miss Hilda Ford, but we call her Fordie. She was with my brother and his family for over thirty years, but then he died and his family had grown up, so she came here. Fordie is of a dying race of people who give up their lives completely to serve others. There used to be people like her in most of the families who could afford servants, but I am afraid that's all gone now. I'm very lucky, though. I know she won't leave, and she will outlive me easily. I've made arrangements so that she will be able to retire and enjoy the rest of her life in comfort. But she is very jealous, so you must be careful."

Our first hours with John were timeless. The conversation was simple. He asked us many questions and told stories from his long relationship with Elizabeth. I wondered why they hadn't married, but I did not want to ask. Occasionally he said something that gave us a hint as to why we had come. I noticed the kindness and thoughtfulness of the way in which he had put us at ease. But Nur was very quiet, and eventually he noticed this.

"Why are you so silent?" he asked, "Elizabeth said you had lots to say. It's no good being shy around me. We haven't got all that much time, and there is much to share."

I noticed then, that Nur was crying. She was looking at John, and tears were rolling down her cheeks. I went to put my arm round her, but she shook her head.

"Couldn't all this suffering have been avoided?" she asked John.

John smiled, "Come on," he said. "It's time for lunch, give me a hand up both of you."

The table was beautifully set with salads, cold cuts, cheese, fruit, and a large jar of black olives. I was just about to ask something about what had happened before lunch when John turned to me.

"Do you like olives?" he asked.

"Yes, very much," I replied. Once again there was that *déjà vu* experience. I was reminded of a day in Turkey when my teacher had said almost the exact words. He had proceeded to teach me how to prepare olives, but it was only later that I had realized he was actually teaching me something about transformation.

"I doctor them myself," John went on. "When we have more time, I must teach you how to do it yourself. I think they taste quite different from the ones you buy in the shops, don't you?"

Over coffee, I told him the story of the olives. He laughed. "It's a small world, isn't it? I read what you wrote about your travels, because Elizabeth had the book and lent it to me. I couldn't help chuckling at the situations you got yourself into! As you gather, I have spent some time in the Middle East myself.

"I used to work for the diplomatic service at one time, so I was able to travel a great deal and had many opportunities to study the dervishes. They were wonderful people. It was perhaps the richest time of my life, being with them! I used to get away for weekends and holidays in the mountains of Iran, Afghanistan, and in North Africa, but for me there were none greater than those who followed the Way of Mevlana Jalalu'ddin Rumi. I know you have studied, so we may be able to get into the subject very deeply.

"It is time that more people in the West understood the meaning of completion, for I believe our time to be a period in history when there is a very real chance that the ancient sciences will be brought to light, and there can be cooperation between the different schools of knowledge. It was so once before in Anatolia, if you remember, at the time of Mevlana, 700 years ago. Perhaps we'll write a book together and see if we can explain something about this in our own language from the experiences we have had. But enough discussion for now. I have a lovely room for you both; and Fordie got flowers in today from the garden.

"She only comes in during the mornings," he said as an aside. "Unless she 'comes all over queer!' as she puts it, and then she rides steaming down the hill from the village on her bicycle. So don't be surprised if she turns up at odd hours. She's normally right in her instincts, as I sometimes get bad cramps and can't manage to wheel myself into the bathroom and all that. Anyway, why don't you rest for a couple of hours? It has been a long drive for you, and I like to have some time to read in the afternoons."

Our room was so beautifully prepared that we both stood in the doorway for several minutes to take it all in. The furnishings were simple but gave such warmth to the space that we felt like familiar guests. A finely crocheted bedspread covered the raised mahogany bed, and an early nineteenth-century dressing table and chair were placed against a wall. A deep armchair with a reading lamp and table faced the door. Two other small occasional tables bearing bowls of red and yellow roses and a large Victorian plant stand stood by the long French windows. I remembered the first sight of John on his veranda, but I had not noticed then that there was another veranda on the other side of the front door.

We walked to the window and looked out at the countryside. Everything was perfectly green. A river threaded its way through the valley, sparkling in the afternoon sunlight. I spotted a man walking down the riverbank, and we could just see the light reflected off his fishing rod as he stopped every now and again and carefully cast his fly into the rising trout. Below, the road up which we had driven moved on to the left, skirting a small wood, and rose up steeply over the brow of the hill.

"God, it's beautiful," Nur said. "But why is there such pain? Look at John, eaten away with cancer, paralyzed and dying while we are whole and have all the work in front of us. I wonder why this happened to a man like him?"

"Why to anyone, I suppose. Perhaps that is what we came to find out. After all what is death? If you consider it, it's not what it appears to be. I had a long think about it last night realizing that a good part of the time we are living, we are half dead anyway, wasting energy in silly arguments and confusion."

Nur became silent again. The sun cast long shadows from the willow trees,

58

and we watched a heron glide down from the wood to take up its position at the edge of a pool. She put her hand on my arm. "Will you make love with me?" she asked.

No one had ever spoken to me in quite that way before. There was a stillness and presence in her manner that allowed me the freedom to love her in a way I had not known before. It was quite a different thing to consciously accept being together in that moment. Time and space were fused in a sense of mutual yearning. Yet it was not a yearning to return to anywhere but where we are. Sentimentality gave way to knowledge, and knowledge to understanding—subtler and subtler energies were transformed. For a brief moment, it was possible to understand the great saying from the Koran, "Wheresoe'r ye look, there is the face of God."

The key was in something I had been told years ago in connection with woman herself—that she is already complete if she can accept that she is truly recognized in love. I had seen Nur from a deeper level of understanding which helped open us both to this other world. She, in her turn, led me on in the play we call love. We were deeply grateful to be alive.

When we came down to the sitting room some time later, we found no sign of John, so we left a brief note and went out, following one of the sheep tracks towards the river. The man was still fishing, but it was getting dark now, and the mist was beginning to rise from the water, spreading back from the bank through the long grass in rapidly moving wisps of cloud. Occasionally a bat darted by in the dusk, squeaking shrilly. We sat and watched until the light was totally gone before walking back to the house.

John was waiting for us in the hall when we arrived. He had moved his chair by the window to watch for us and was just lighting his pipe with the kind of old-fashioned lighter that was designed to strike even in the strongest gale. The effect, however, was a minor bonfire with every suck on the pipe. Clouds of tobacco smoke rose into the air, obscuring John and showering a fine spray of sparks over his clothes. I could not help laughing.

"What's wrong," he asked. "Oh, I see, it's the smoke. I'm sorry about the habit, but smoking is my particular vice. If it really offends you, however, I'll do my best not to smoke when you're around, but frankly I have no reason to give it up at this stage of my life. Fordie gets fed up with me, as I do sometimes forget about the ash, but she puts up with it."

We both interrupted him by saying that of course we didn't mind about the smoking. It was just the minor volcano in his pipe that had made us laugh. I was reminded however, of my surprise when I first went to the Middle East and found that nearly all my teachers and spiritual guides smoked heavily. The longstanding image I had had of highly ascetic spiritual teachers was simply not so.

John smiled when I told him this. "You know," he said, "I have an intuition that it is not smoking alone that causes lung cancer but fear and smoking together. I may be wrong in this but I do know for certain that fear coupled with guilt can most certainly increase the mental chaos from which cancer emanates."

"So far as I understand it," he said, "cancer is merely a manifestation of chaos." Having read my thoughts, John paused briefly. "You will probably ask why I got cancer? It's obviously not so simple, is it? Things cannot always be explained logically. Perhaps a serious illness is destiny at work, and nothing can be said about it; perhaps mistakes we have made in the past are producing an inner sense of guilt that can emerge in the manifested world years later as a form of illness.

"The first thing, however, is not to be frightened. That is how I can live with the cancer I have. Certainly it is painful, but I have worked and worked not to allow myself to be brought down to the state of chaos in which the pain takes over and consciousness is lost. If we lose consciousness, we are asleep and miss the beauty of life.

"I don't know whether Elizabeth told you," he said, changing the subject, "but I have a very short time to live."

Nur and I were shocked to be reminded of it. John seemed so alive it seemed impossible to imagine his death as imminent.

"You two are not to worry," he went on. "Remember why you have come. Life is too precious a gift to waste in limitation or in lack of awareness of all that is being taught and given each moment. I have no fear of death, for I know that there is no such thing. If anything, it has only enabled me to live life even more fully. I have no regrets.

"It is harder to understand when you're young, but one day everyone has to remember; the earlier the better, in many ways. Isn't that right?" He smiled.

We were silent for a moment. Nur spoke. "But how did it start, John?" she said, touching his hand.

"It is a long story," he replied. "I don't know all the answers even now, and perhaps it is irrelevant. Suffice it to say that I developed a malignant growth in my left shoulder a little over eight years ago, and about a year after I became paralyzed." He paused and drew heavily on his pipe. We sat in silence. "But perhaps there is a lesson to be learned," he said, finally, "from hearing the story itself. But first let's have supper, as I'm sure you're still recovering from your drive."

He led the way into the dining room. A bottle of claret was already opened, and the food was warming on the hotplate. Unlike the first meal we had shared together, John remained mostly in silence. He said that he preferred not to speak at the evening meal if possible and that he would tell the story afterwards.

Over coffee, he began. "You will have noticed the objects from the Middle East I have in the house," he said. "I am not worried about possessions anymore, but each one of them tells a story. I notice the objects, rugs, furniture, and photographs and am reminded of the lessons that needed to be learned at the time. I consciously remember so that I do not forget again. It is an art to recollect an experience in past time, knowing that in reality there is no such thing, and to bring the experience into present time in a useful form. The key is relatively simple, and that is that we are continuously being given experiences, out of which we can learn. Once understood, we do not need the experience anymore. Perhaps the greatest teacher and lesson of all is life itself; but I am digressing.

"Just after the war, I inherited a little money. The world was split in two then: into those who were trying to pick up the pieces and those who were surging ahead with objective hope. I was one of the latter. I was quite young. During the war, I fought in the desert in North Africa, and a friend and I had decided to retrace our steps with the Eighth Army. War brings people very closely together, and now when the promised peace had come we shared a bond that we felt could never be broken. We had gone through so much together and seen so many of our brothers blown to bits in the desert or trapped in their burning tanks, while we, somehow or other, came out physically unscathed. Emotionally, we were all shot to pieces after those years, as the scars of war take time to heal, but we were some of the lucky ones, and the journey we had decided to take was in some ways a pilgrimage. We had no idea at the outset how radically our well-laid plans would be altered."

John lit his pipe again and gazed into the fire. We eventually got used to his silences, but it was somewhat disconcerting at first. Sometimes the stillness was only broken when he pushed himself out of the room, leaving us quite alone. He was not eccentric and he was perfectly mannered, but John was able to go into worlds that interpenetrated the one we normally see. These different worlds are in fact different rates of vibration; the formative worlds of thought, ideas and archetypes that mould much of our own thought, action and feeling. We learned not to disturb him.

But this time he continued: "We started in Tangier. We had decided to buy a good jeep and then to wend our way slowly through Morocco. The country was a smuggler's paradise. It was a centre of trade; there was nothing that you couldn't obtain. I was offered everything from dope and young girls to an unlimited number of second-hand tanks! People made a fortune during that period. They bought up all the war equipment they could salvage, for the sake of its metal. It was a strange alchemy, converting base metals, in a manner of speaking, into gold.

"Anyway, the first part of the journey went off well enough, but matters changed in a small Moroccan village. My friend had been very interested in the world of Islam, and as the war ended he met a man called Yussaf Ali, who had invited him to come and stay with his family in this little village. We did not want to miss the opportunity, so we sent a letter in advance and decided to go for a couple of days.

"We were warmly greeted, spoiled rotten with food and kindness, so that it became increasingly hard for us to leave. Finally, after three days of festivity, we were introduced to an old woman who was very important in the village.

"Her husband had been the local wise man—some sort of a sheikh, I believe—but he had recently died. Her son lived with her, and, although young, he was destined, we were told, to step into his father's shoes. We didn't know it then, but our coming had fulfilled a prophecy, and we had not been in the house for more than a few minutes of formality and mint tea when the old lady turned to us and announced that she wanted us to stay on with her in the village. "I have been waiting for you," she said, "for twenty years."

"Now, what would you have done," John asked smiling at me. "Knowing the type of person you are, it would not have been possible to resist the offer, would it?"

I was so caught up by the story that I suspect I would have accepted, as John had said. I had never been one to reject an adventure.

"I feel a bit chilled," John said. "Perhaps if you could put more logs on the fire and fetch me a small whisky, we could continue a bit longer. My shoulder is very painful at this time of the evening, and I have to change the dressing on the wound before I go to bed."

"I could help you, John," Nur said. "I used to know a little about nursing."

"Don't worry, my dear," he said. "I can manage quite well, and after all you have only been here for a day. Wait a little and then we will see."

I went outside to get the logs from the shed. In the garden, I stopped for a moment to collect myself. It was hard to remember that we had come to Wales only this morning. It was dark outside. There were no stars and I couldn't find an outside light. The shock of nearly falling over the woodpile returned me to my senses; I finally managed to get myself together enough to carry the logs back into the house.

"Sorry I was so long," I said. "The normal sequence of time just doesn't seem to apply when I'm listening to stories like this. It's quite disturbing."

"You will have to remember what I said about learning from experience," he replied, "and then perhaps you will begin to see how time works. Now, where was I? Oh yes, back in the village.

"Naturally, I could not resist the offer, but my friend ironically, was much more skeptical, and after much arguing he decided to go on, taking the jeep with him. He agreed to pick me up in two and a half weeks, but he was very upset. I kept pointing out to him that opportunities like this did not come along very often, but he couldn't see it. I wish now I had listened to him, particularly since a similar thing had happened once before. I had let him down by breaking my word, and I finally got myself into a lot of trouble. That is something that I hope both of you will not forget, always question your motives and never be vague about fulfilling what you have said you will do, for every time you break your word or deviate from your course, for whatever reason, you are liable to lose a little will, so that finally you lose the power of discriminating the right action at the right moment.

"So I stayed on. Many things were given, and many of them became useful to me and to others later in life, but there came a time when something told me that it was time to leave. I felt I could not absorb anymore, and the family was becoming more and more possessive. The date for the rendezvous was very near, so I thought I could wait until my friend came and then leave with him. But the day he was due to arrive the old lady summoned me into her room. She told me that she wanted me to go into a cave with her son for eighteen days. I answered that I felt it was time for me to go. She became angrier when I reiterated that I was going to leave, and, shaking her fist under my nose, she shouted, eyes blazing, "You promised to stay!" I pointed out that I had not said exactly how long, but her fury remained unabated. I was in such a state of fear that I tightened in that moment. I realized then, that I was not prepared to really commit myself even though I said I would rather naively in the beginning. I prayed under my breath that the jeep would arrive at that moment. But it didn't. It did not come for another eight days by which time I had developed a high fever and was really ill. When my friend finally arrived, he insisted we go back to Tangier immediately to see a doctor at the hospital. The old lady refused to see us off.

"I was taken to the hospital and developed this paralysis. The doctors argued and argued. Some said it was polio and others that it was a tropical disease, but the fact remained that I lost the use of my legs.

"There is no need to read anything more into the story than what I have said." He smiled at us, and I detected a twinkle in his eyes.

"But how did the cancer develop, John?" I started.

"Let's stop for tonight, I am tired now. What you can do is help me upstairs. I have put a steel runner on the side of the staircase. Let me show you. It's a marvelous invention!"

He wheeled his chair to the bottom of the stairs. I noticed that there were connecting rods under the arms of the chair that fitted into the steel runners. When they were fixed in place, he pressed a switch, and his chair started to move up the stairs. With a little help from behind, he was soon at the top. "Good night," he said, "I am delighted to have you here. It will fulfill my own destiny and perhaps help you towards your own. Sleep well. God bless you." Nur went forward to kiss him, but he had already turned his chair round and was going into his room. It was the first time that I noticed the appalling smell of the cancer.

I tossed and turned all that night. John's story had been oddly disquieting. I wondered exactly what he was trying to tell us. Surely I had broken my promises a thousand times, but so far with nothing so dramatic happening as the events he had described. I am not a heavy sleeper at the best of times, but that night I was particularly uncomfortable. It was not fear I felt, but there were so many questions, questions concerning the nature of destiny, fate, willpower, and chance. There were too many to let me sleep. Finally, I crept out of bed and sat by the window, with the reading light on beside me. Nur was sleeping deeply. I read a section called "The Lover's Immortality" from one of the volumes of the Mathnawi, the book of Mevlana Jallalu'ddin Rumi. Two couplets were especially significant to me at that time: "Thou didst bestow on me a spiritual/death and a resurrection continually" and "Reason is trembling with fear of death/but Love is bold."

I must have fallen asleep sitting up in the chair, for I awoke with a start. It was already light, and when I looked back to the bed I saw that Nur had gone. For a moment, I panicked. It was the same sensation as being granted a taste of incredible beauty and then suddenly returning to the same old rut. Years later, Nur had a terrible car accident. Someone telephoned me from the site. They did not know whether she would live, and it was going to take me four hours to get to the hospital where she had been taken. It was the same panic this time. We have so little trust. We fear that something or someone is going to be taken away. "Trust, trust," my teacher used to say to me. "Why won't you trust?"

The shock brought back many memories of my confusion when I simply did not understand what my teacher was getting at. I could understand trusting "in" something that was tangible or that I had realized through personal experience to be true, but to trust something beyond any concept was a different matter altogether! I did finally understand what was being said to me, however. I realized that trusting in something far greater than ourselves, a divine plan, if you like, was only possible if we trusted and then perhaps finally knew, that God is perfect. Thus, each moment is perfect in essence. We could trust in this and work with it. What we often think to be trust is our ability to change something that already exists, and that was what Elizabeth was driving at when she talked about the three walls that divide us from truth, the walls of resentment, envy, and pride.

I sat watching the darkness lighten to a pale grey. The rain was coming down in a fine drizzle that would probably stop in an hour or two. I could hardly see the river, but sensed its beauty through the mist. I heard a dog bark and a man's voice calling to the cows. Shadowy figures passed by in single file through the gate just below the house and turned up the hill toward the near-by farm. It was the time of the dawn chorus, and the air was filled with bird-song. The creak of the gate drew my attention, and I saw Nur coming up the pathway. In the sudden relief, I felt rather foolish for my fantasies. She was wearing rubber boots and jeans with a heavy Irish sweater to keep out the damp. Her dark hair hung almost to her waist. It was quite wet. I watched her bend her head down and a little to one side, taking the hair in her hands and shaking out the moisture.

"Hullo," I said, looking down from the bedroom window. "Did you have a good walk? For a while I thought you had packed your bags and disap-peared."

"Don't be ridiculous," she said, smiling.

Shortly, Nur came upstairs. Stripping off the heavy sweater, she lay on the bed beside me. "It's so beautiful out there. The early morning is an incredibly special time. Night thoughts have gone to sleep, and the thoughts of the day have not yet fully awakened. I love it. When I'm in the country, I always try to get up at dawn. You can see things so clearly then. Do you remember quoting me the words like Ibn el Arabi, "All is contained in the Divine Breath like the day in the morning's dawn?" Well, that is what I felt this morning. It seemed that with preparation we could indeed set the pattern for the day. The breath-ing that we learned in Turkey helped me more perhaps than anything else to return to a state of order."

"Do you really understand why we were given that rhythm?" I asked her.

"Yes, I think I can say something about it now. Do you remember we were given the rhythm first without any real explanation? I feel that was done ini-tially so that we could come to understand something of ourselves. Although, when something did happen for me later, I was still unable to talk about it. But what do you think?" she asked.

"Well, obviously the rhythm of 7-1-7-1-7 has something to do with the musical octave. To breathe in to the count of seven, pause for one, and then breathe out again to the count of seven before pausing once more to repeat the cycle brings in a steady rhythm. The benefit has been enormous for me as well, and I have practiced it ever since it was given. But I've never understood why it should be called the Mother's Breath."

Nur puzzled a moment. "You know," she answered, "when I was mad it was terrifying, because the only reality I had were my illusions. In my fear, I wondered what would happen if they all went. Would there be anything of 'me' left? But all that time I was continuously encouraged to practice that rhythm, to follow the breath in and out, to be 'on top of it.' And little by little I became calm. Sometimes I could even see what lay within the moment. I remember writing in my notebook that "The moment contains the womb of possibilities." So perhaps the Mother's Breath helps us to see the infinite possibility lying in the here and now. It's like the physical womb, isn't it? Does that make any sense?"

Nur leant over and laid her head on my chest. We both listened to the rhythm: seven counts, pause, seven counts, pause. Her rhythm and my own were the same. There was a blending together that took us rapidly into a state of harmony and gentleness. We lay there for a while, hardly daring to speak.

Then I said, "The rhythm of the breathing that we were given was to help us to see that the present moment *pulsates*, expanding and contracting, coming into existence and passing out of it again instantaneously. Everything is born from this rhythmic pulsation of 'the womb of the moment,' as you've called it, Nur. The rhythm also produces the waves of vibration that makes up the subtle or formative worlds interpenetrating the grosser physical substance. It's all a question of different rates of vibration: the slower the rate, the denser the material; the higher the rate of vibration the more refined and less stable the substance."

"Yes, that's it!" she said sitting up excitedly. "And the rate of pulsation is the same as the rhythm of the breath, 7-1-7. Do you remember what Plato said? I can't remember the exact words but he was implying that it was our human knowledge of the musical octave that kept things in balance and harmony."

We were both very excited now, for a whole new world was opening up. If all this about the womb of the moment and the rate of its pulsation were true, then birth, sex, and death, the three acts that can be made in consciousness to help bring about real change, could be seen to be in one moment. Perhaps this pulsation is what it's all about. Perhaps this is what stands between the world of time and eternity itself. I remembered being told, with great force, that it was necessary for humanity to know these three acts on quite a different level. I had even been told that before the knowledge was forgotten many of the women who had given birth to extraordinary children had been to special schools where they learned how to prepare themselves for conscious birth. It had been suggested, for example, that the mother of Alexander the Great had attended such a school. Already being with Nur had opened up so many things in these few days.

We spent a long time lying on the bed talking. Both of us had, in our own individual ways, come on similar intuitions, so the flow between us was overwhelming. A whole new way of living seemed possible. If "Everything is contained in the Divine Breath like the day in the morning's dawn," then, with this knowledge, this breath, this rhythm, we could surely be of service to the divine order on quite another scale.

We nearly got carried away by theories just then, but Nur noticed in time. "Come on," she said, pulling me to my feet, "I can't take too much more of this now, and anyway it's time for breakfast. But it's a whole new situation, isn't it? I mean—you *can* see the possibilities of our being together?"

"Now you're the one who's talking too much!" I teased.

John was not awake yet, but the smell of bacon and eggs wafted from the kitchen, and Fordie soon appeared, wiping her hands on a cloth.

"I'm afraid that Mr. John's not feeling too well today, sir," she said. "So please help yourselves to whatever you want. I'm going to take him his breakfast in bed. He asked me to tell you to make yourselves comfortable, and he will come down later. You do know that he's a very sick man, don't you, sir? The doctor spoke with me just the other day about it, and we are doing our best to make his life as comfortable as possible. He does get overtired very easily, but he loves talking to people like you. I can't stop him, although I scold him sometimes for his own good."

Nur and I spent a long time over breakfast. More and more we began to understand that we had been sent to John to experience what it could mean to die consciously. This concept alone touched on some huge subjects, particularly on the nature of healing. We realized that real healing has to do with the removal of all that stands between us and the truth. In that light, most so-called healing could be seen as very subtle forms of therapy, emotional, or psychological. The journey we were all taking by being alive could never be said to be painless or, indeed, easy, but with people like John, Elizabeth, and my own teacher in Turkey, we could begin, little by little, to see our way.

In John's presence, we experienced a continuous overflowing of love that demanded nothing for itself. In the time we spent with him we discovered that it was not so much what he said but what was carried with his words in every breath that helped to lead us on, almost relentlessly, toward our own freedom together, freedom from the fear of loss.

Some years later, someone asked me, "What are we? Who are we? What is the purpose of life?" I could only reply from what I had learned in that short time with John: "What I am, what anyone is, is merely a memory pattern to be erased in this lifetime. Who I am cannot be answered in any words that would fit the mind; and it is our obligation to question and make whatever sacrifice necessary to discover the purpose of life on earth."

9

When we saw John later that morning, he was very grey and seemed weak. Fordie wheeled him about and finally brought him out onto the veranda. The rain had gone, leaving all the promise of a beautiful spring day. It was warm in the sunlight, and John was comfortable with just a light blanket around his shoulders.

"I love it out here," he said, "I find it easier to meditate in the open air. It's a paradox, for I contemplate on the permanence of truth in the presence of all the beauty of the perishable, sitting here and watching the seasons change year after year. But perhaps it is also possible to see it here. After all, what did Blake say? 'To see eternity in a grain of sand, and heaven in a wildflower.' It's harder when you are young to live with that degree of passion, just as it is harder to live in certain other ways when you are old.

"Anyway," he went on, "this morning I felt it was time to talk to you about certain things, so try to listen carefully."

"But John," I ventured, "Fordie says that you are not well today, and we don't want to exhaust you."

"No, no," he interrupted. "It is my pleasure to have you here! All I want to do is to complete our conversation of last night—about the cancer, I mean. Probably, because I was to some degree locked in that moment of fear when the old woman shook her fist in fury at my lack of will, or for some reason I do not know, a growth developed on the left side of my chest and spread through into the shoulder, sometimes immobilizing most of my left arm. It is not a pleasant sight, but that shouldn't bother us either. The doctors took tests and over a period of years did their best with operations, chemotherapy, the lot. I think I always knew that it was hopeless, it was my destiny if you like, and so I did my best not to miss a breath. By the time this old body collapsed, I wanted there to be nothing but love, no anger or hate, no resentment or bitterness, and, most of all, no regrets. I wished to spend the rest of my life being grateful for being alive.

"You know," he continued, "we stand continuously between what we call life and what we call death. For those who find a reality in chasing after endless physical pleasures, wealth, and possessions, the very thought of the death of the physical body is put so far back into the subconscious that they miss the chance of being free in life. They smother the possibility of freedom by surrounding themselves in more and more protection in the forms of the physical world. If children were only brought up with the joy that lies in the challenge of life, there would be much less fear in the world, and more people would live in the present. We *can* overcome death. Joy can be as infectious as the diseases that end the physical life span; it is fear and guilt that block the avenues to true freedom."

"These are tremendously high ideals, John," I said. "And not many people come to the depth of understanding that you have."

John smiled, "Perhaps not yet," he replied. "But if you consider, both of you, your own personal search and the yearning behind it, is it just by chance that you have met up with circumstances that led you here? You must know, by now, that there is no such thing as chance. The trouble is that you take experience for granted and do not see that each experience is a stepping-stone toward freedom. If you could only accept whatever comes in gratefulness!

"Think about it," John said, turning to me, "haven't you wanted to know about sex? Haven't you wanted to know about the inner meaning of birth, and of death? Come on now. If you hadn't had the inner yearning, you wouldn't be in this situation now. After all, look at it. You have Nur, who may become your partner in life and through whom you might gain some knowledge of what lies behind the act of sex and of birth. And now you are both here with me. Can you see, after all these years, that everything is provided as soon as we ask the question? Jesus said, 'Seek and ye shall find.' Do you remember?"

Just at that moment, the telephone rang. I felt a great sense of relief as I went to answer it.

It was a woman's voice on the line. "My name is Margaret," she said, "you must be John's friend. Welcome to Wales. John has told me all sorts of nice things about you both, and I hope that you will come over for tea and see the garden. But how is John? I had a strange dream about him and had to call."

"Who is it?" shouted John, from the veranda.

"It's Margaret," I said. "She is asking how you are."

"Tell her I'm fine, and that I'm being looked after very well. And tell her that she worries too much!"

I heard Margaret laugh on the other end of the phone. "He's incorrigible," she said, "but I'm happy to hear that he's OK. Anyway, please do come and see me, or perhaps I'll pop by later today or tomorrow." She rang off, and I heard the click of the receiver being put down.

"Who was that?" I asked John after I had sat down again.

"That was Margaret, a very good friend of mine," he explained. "She is involved with all manner of healing and perhaps you will have a chance to meet later. But for the time being, I want to continue our conversation without being sidetracked. Please get me a glass of sherry from the dining room, will you? And have one yourselves," he called after us, "then we can go on."

There was something inexorable in the way that John spoke to us that morning, however tired he was. I noticed on more than one occasion a sense of agitation in his voice as he tried to explain certain points. He would lean forward in his chair, staring deeply at one of us to make a point clear, or would wave his pipe frustratedly in the air if we were not paying sufficient attention. Both of us realized that he was attempting to transmit ideas that, in many ways, were far beyond us to understand at the time.

"As I told you," he continued, "I had a letter from Elizabeth, who in turn had received a letter from your teacher in Turkey. I also had a very long conversation on the telephone with her just before you arrived. We discussed many things, mainly to do with what it seemed you both wanted to understand at this time. But now perhaps we can go a little further.

"Have either of you ever considered that ideas alone can change a human being? The transmission of ideas comes from a higher world than the one that we experience with the senses or even touch on with the rational mind. The world of ideas is a world on its own, linking up with us only when we agree to it and work with it in a special way." He stopped for a moment to watch us. "Many of the things I wish to give you will be new," he explained. "Others will be familiar—but either way it is important to listen as though for the first time. Otherwise, your minds will try to compare and the result will be limited."

"I understand what you are saying, John," Nur replied. "There was a time when I could see that other world. Each idea was a shape that could be understood, rather than seen with the eyes. There even seemed to be a hierarchy of shape and an ordered system to it all. Is that right?"

"Yes—in a way. But not everyone has the same experiences as you, and for our conversation to work we will have to keep pace with each other.

"The way to approach this is to look into the meaning of the *conscious*. People bandy this word around a great deal, but few have the slightest idea of its real meaning. We can say, for instance, the word sex, and it would not be hard to conjure up a variety of descriptions relating to the word, but if we were to say *conscious sex*, or *conscious birth*, or *conscious death*, we would have added a whole new dimension to things. Language is such an important subject. It is meant to be a means of communication, not merely a tool for intellectual reasoning. Language was never intended to feed the gossiping mind, but rather was meant to be understood as a vast pattern system, each language producing different patterns in order to communicate ideas across time and space.

"All right, then, let us return to this word *conscious*. According to some dictionaries, it means being awake to the moment or sharing another's knowledge of awareness. But that doesn't seem a sufficient explanation as far as I am concerned. It is true that to be conscious we have to be awake; and it is also true to say that most of our lives we can notice, if we are quite honest with ourselves, that we are unconscious, and thus asleep. As G. I. Gurdjieff said so often, we are 'sleepwalkers.'

"If I give you a big nudge in the ribs," he said to me, puffing so hard at his pipe that smoke billowed from the bowl, "would you be able to say, at this precise moment, that you were awake? Be honest with me."

Nur smiled, "You know," she said. "I just happened to be watching you when John spoke. You had the most extraordinary glazed look in your eyes."

It was quite true. I really was somewhere else. I had heard the words that John was speaking, but most certainly they had not sunk in. I could hear them still floating around somewhere, as it were, but there was so much in what he was saying that it was hard to listen with sufficient attention.

"It is the mind again," John said. "Either you were trying to compare one idea with another, which cannot work, or you were sensing that you were not capable of understanding. The last would be ridiculous, since I would not talk about these things if I did not know that both of you could understand and that the ideas would continue to grow in you over many years. Let's go back to this point of being awake.

"Our recognition that we are asleep, unawake, and thus unconscious of what is really going on serves as an impetus for us to begin to find out what it could mean to be truly conscious, living human beings, not half-human creatures swayed by every outside force, everyone else's moods, and even the changes in the weather. Thus if we could be completely conscious at the time of birth, life could be seen quite differently, couldn't it?

"We've all heard about the natural childbirth movement. Well, personally I don't like the expression, for is not childbirth perfectly natural in the first place? It is true that, through drugs and so on, we have made it very unnatural, but just because a woman does not take drugs and has her baby at home does not mean to say that either she or her husband are actually *conscious*. To be conscious is a very high state indeed and needs much work to come to the realization of the true meaning of the word. If the parents were really conscious they would be participating in the creation of space for the manifestation of eternal recurrence.

"Now *that* might take some considering," John said laughing. "Do you think that space just happens on its own, and human beings have little, or nothing to do with it? That subject alone could make a book. However, I did say I would give you ideas, not books! But look at it quite simply. When you construct a building, you are working with space, are you not? In the same way, if you visualize a shape, you are also involved with creating space. Now imagine what the understanding of this could mean when it comes to conscious birth. A whole world opens up. If the child that is born *knows*, without any shadow of a doubt, that he or she is loved and that both the physical and psychic space into which it is born is in conscious order, then we have gone a long way to helping that being come into the world.

"Once again, we have to look at the idea—that being awake is a prerequisite to being conscious and that, since the future of our planet lies in the hands of the children, it is really our obligation to be conscious at the moment of birth whether it be our own children, ourselves, or the world that is coming into being anew with each breath. All this requires real effort on our part. It just doesn't happen on its own. Do you see what I am getting at?"

I was about to say something when John closed his eyes and took a slow, deep breath. The air became still, and I was aware of sounds I had not heard before. I heard the bees working in the flowers, bordering the veranda, the birds calling in the valley, the wind rustling the leaves, a dog barking in the distance, and the faint sound of some children playing; it seemed that I could hear them *all at once*. It was an extraordinary experience, for I realized, at that moment, that normally it only appears that we hear, or see, more than one thing at a time. Perhaps for a brief moment I knew the meaning of consciousness as a form of energy, for it was possible to realize that all the sounds were taking different lengths of time to reach my ears, and thus to hear them all at once it was necessary to transcend space and time as we normally perceive it. In the same way, what we appear to see is already gone! The light of the sun takes eight minutes to reach us, so when we look at the sun we are seeing it where it was eight minutes before. We see light from stars that no longer exist. Even a leaf is not the same as it appears to be, because it has already changed by the time it reaches our perception. It is merely a memory pattern.

John opened his eyes and continued to breathe deeply. "You had a taste?" he said. "Never think, my friend; instead, *use* thought. It is a form of energy, and it will serve you and open your eyes to many things."

I was in such a state that I wondered if I could listen to much more. I realized that I had taken a step in that experience and that I could not return to my previous state. To be conscious had become both an overwhelming desire and a necessity.

"Where was I?" John said, questioning himself good-naturedly. "Ah, yes—this business about being conscious. I'm only going to give you one or two more ideas, so that you don't get indigestion. These you can mull over, and perhaps we will have time to talk more about them later. We've touched on the notion of conscious birth, but what about conscious sex? However odd this may sound, it is very much harder than we might imagine. If you think about it, most people go to sleep the moment they make love! Forgive me if that sounds outrageous, but it's true. Women are sometimes more aware of this than men, aren't they, Nur?" he said.

"Sex is considered to be the most sacred act on earth, and thus should be treated accordingly. At the very least, we are asked to be conscious in making love. That means that we have to be awake and in a similar state to that which you have just experienced. Thus, preparation is necessary on all levels, from physical cleanliness to the higher levels of breath and discipline of the mind. If we are awake and conscious of the divine, who provides everything for us, sex can become sacred. It is not given for the procreation of the species alone, nor is it just for release. Conscious sex transforms energies, and since God made us in His image, we have much to explore here. As I said, you can consider these ideas, and deepen your understanding of them throughout the years. Once the seeds have been sown, there is the chance of real understanding.

"You must have patience, however. As Mevlana says, 'Patience is the key to joy' and 'Gratefulness is the key to will.' Don't expect to understand all these things overnight. Everything in this world takes time. Patience is not a passive state, as so many people assume, but an actively receptive one that needs to be cultivated. Patience is something that you must work on, as it is not as easy as it sounds.

"If I wish to plant a peach tree, for example, I must prepare the soil carefully before planting. It will be several years before the tree is capable of bearing fruit, but I cannot leave it at that and do nothing, can I? I need to see that the tree is pruned regularly and that it is protected from animals that might wish to eat its bark and from insects that wish to devour its leaves. In time the young tree will grow strong and healthy. When it blossoms, the weather must be watched carefully for frost. When the fruit appears, it must be protected from wasps and from people who might try to pick the fruit before it is ripe. Eventually, I would have a peach, ready to eat, which was the cause of the peach tree being planted in the first place.

"It is the same with ideas. They need to be sown, and the person to whom they are given must be sufficiently prepared that the ideas do not fall on untended soil. If we remain in a passive state after the seeds of an idea have been sown, it will be a miracle if anything grows. Like the peach tree, ideas must be actively tended to grow into something really useful.

"To be conscious takes a lot of patience and hard work. It does not come at once, nor is it 'given' to us in a passive state of doing nothing. No one else can do it for us. We have to make the efforts, and then we are given all the rules of the game. Don't let your minds wander. I am still talking about conscious sex, if you could only see it! Keep to the theme.

"You were told that you needed to know about woman," he said to me, "isn't that true? The word matrix was used several times. If you apply your question to the subject, something may come out of it for both of you.

"Let me try to explain it this way. If we can see that the womb of the moment is a matrix, or blueprint for infinite possibilities, then the womb of a woman is the physical manifestation of this, also containing infinite possibilities. If the sexual act is a loving and fully conscious act, then the being that may be conceived depends heavily on the parents' degree of consciousness. Don't misunderstand, for this is a very subtle point. If you *try* to be more conscious, you will only feed a concept, not an idea, and you will thus build your own ego. All that can be done actually is to work through sacrifice and surrender to be a more fitting vehicle for grace."

"But, John," I said, "it is not as though a child is conceived each time someone makes love. What about the other times? Where does consciousness fit in there?"

"Ah," said John puffing at his pipe once again. "Ah! Now that is the sort of question I like. It means that something is happening within you. Now, what is a child? It, too, is not what it appears to be. Did I not say that a child is the *manifestation* of eternal recurrence? That is the physical child, but what about the children of ideas? What about conscious evolution of the planet, rather than just organic evolution? Supposing we humans have a very definite role to play in evolution and that evolution becomes conscious to the degree that we make the necessary efforts and become conscious ourselves? What if I were to say that conscious sex releases certain energies that can very directly bear on evolution itself, whether a physical child is conceived or not? Could you accept that?"

Nur slipped her hand in mine. She sensed the confusion that I was going through, since just about everything that I had thought before in connection with sex was starting to mean little, if anything, after what John had said.

"I think it's easier for women to understand," Nur said. "Most men have to turn inward to let understanding enter, by being totally receptive instead of going out for the meaning. Do you remember reading me the words of Jesus in the Gospel of Thomas when we were in Turkey?

When you make the two one, and when you make the inner as the outer and the outer as the inner and the above as the below, and when you make the male and the female into a single one, so that the male will not be male and the female (not) be female . . .then shall you enter (the Kingdom).

"Well it's something like that, isn't it?" she asked turning to John.

"That is it exactly!" he replied. "Heaven is the perfection lying within the invisible matrix from which all comes. The Kingdom of Heaven is there, all the time, but we have to be receptive to it. It cannot be found by chasing after it. In a sense, everything is upside-down, and there must be a complete transformation within us to understand these things.

"But I'm tired," he said. "I haven't talked so much in years. When the time is right, we will be able to complete this conversation by going into the meaning of conscious death. However, for the time being please don't discuss anything with each other. Just let the ideas sink in. I tell you what, why don't you take a drive and have lunch out? Just enjoy yourselves. I'm not hungry just now anyway. Come on; help me inside out of the wind. It's getting chilly."

We pushed John into his study. Grey clouds were scudding over the valley, damping the patches of sunshine. It looked as if it might rain again. I stacked several pieces of wood in the fireplace and lit the fire for John, as he was looking pale. A pile of books rested on the table beside him, but he didn't seem to notice. As I turned back at the door, I saw that his head was already nodding.

10

We drove up the road to our left, as John had directed us. It was a five-minute drive to the village, which lay half hidden by trees in a fold of the hill. Time stood still in the village. Nothing ever seemed to have changed. In these small villages, the local shops were the centre of activity. Everything was still served by hand, often from a single shop. The postmistress had only to take two steps from the post office grill to serve you with all the fresh eggs, locally cured bacon, and staple provisions you could ever need. There was very little that could not be learned in the village shops.

We stopped to see if we could find a gift to bring back to John. It was hard not to discuss what he had been telling us, but there was obviously a reason why he had asked us to keep quiet. "Don't think," he had said, "but use thought consciously." Ironically, I was soon thinking just what that could mean.

"It's hard not to think, isn't it?" I asked Nur as we looked around the shop.

"Well, just don't," she answered tersely. "Anyway, let's consider what we are going to get John." We found ourselves arguing almost at once. I suggested flowers, as there were multicolored bunches of dahlias that would have looked wonderful in John's study. "That's a bit ridiculous!" Nur said. "What's the point in giving him flowers when the garden is full of them?"

"Well, I didn't see any inside other than those in our bedroom."

"Obviously, then, if he wanted them he would ask Fordie to pick enough for every room in the house. Why would he want cut flowers?"

"All right, then let's not buy flowers, but it's not as though you have made a suggestion yourself," I responded testily, getting cross. "Why don't you make your mind up and decide what you want to buy? I've said what I thought was right."

I noticed that the postmistress was eyeing us carefully from behind the counter. From experience, I guessed what was coming, so I answered her unspoken question.

"We're staying with Mr. John," I said. "Perhaps you can help us. We want to take him a gift but we're having some trouble deciding what to buy. What do you suggest?"

"Well, I tell you what," she answered in her lilting Welsh accent. "Mr. John loves those cheddar cheeses in the basket over there. They are made on a farm in the West Country, but they're difficult to get these days. Miss Ford came in asking for one only yesterday but we were out of stock. One of those little roundels is just two to three pounds, so it isn't very expensive."

"Would you like that, Nur?" I asked her. "Or have you got some other suggestion?"

"Why don't you just buy what you want," she said.

"Don't you worry, miss. I know that it is difficult to choose, but you can be quite sure that Mr. John will be heartily pleased."

Nur smiled ruefully then, and took the cheese. She also chose a freshly baked loaf of bread, still warm from the oven, and brought it over to be wrapped. "I'm sorry," she said, "it's been a difficult day."

"I suppose Mr. John has been telling you all his famous stories," said the postmistress. "He's lived here for a long while now, but he doesn't get out much. It must be difficult being crippled. They say he had an accident or something, but he never said much about it, even when he could get about in his wheelchair. If you ask Miss Ford, she just shuts up and won't say anything either, so we keep quiet about it. Here, take another one of these loaves of bread to him from me, and tell him we were asking after him."

We left the shop and walked across the square to the pub, the smell of fresh bread under our noses. Inside, there was one tiny bar and an adjoining room where five men were sitting round a table playing dominoes. We sat down at a corner table and ordered two pints of bitter.

"Has it ever occurred to you to look at this situation," I said to Nur. "Here we are living with a dying man as though everything was perfectly normal; we are asked not to think about it or anything else, let alone to have a discussion; and we haven't even begun to sort out our mutual future if there really is to be one. Furthermore . . ."

"For heaven's sake," Nur said laughing. "What more could you want than what is happening? Since I've been with Elizabeth, I've learned to accept things as they are, even if they appeared half mad at times; for everything is complete in itself, if we could only understand it. Of course, the situation seems unreal at times, but there is still a sense in it all from which to learn. All we have to do is to accept that we are here and that we may even be actors in this play. I think the reason John asked us not to discuss all this business about being conscious was because you or I, or both of us, were liable to take it all too seriously. What he said was deeply significant, but there is a funny side to it too. Have you thought about how we are going to make love consciously, for example?"

"For heaven's sake, Nur." I was getting quite embarrassed, and I was certain that at least one of the men playing dominoes was listening to our conversation.

"What does it matter if people hear?" asked Nur, sensing my concern. "They would probably think it's ridiculous. And it is! Just imagine how we are going to get our act together on all the levels that John mentioned. By the time we concentrated on all the necessary things, we would probably forget what we were there for!"

Luckily, the pub door opened at that moment, as I was certain Nur was not about to be deterred from the present trend of the conversation. A woman came toward us. Her presence reminded me a little of Elizabeth. She was about the same age, but her appearance physically was quite different. She was tall and her height was accentuated by a long raincoat that reached the top of her Wellington boots.

"Hullo," she said, stretching out her hand. "I'm Margaret, the person you spoke to on the phone. John sent me to find you. He guessed you'd be here. Mind you, there isn't another pub for ten miles. He suggested we all have lunch together at the house and that you were probably talking too much!" Her expression was mischievous. "I'll join you if I may; I could do with a beer myself before we go."

She sat down next to us, unbuttoning her coat. "Whew! It's hot. I've just walked up the hill. How is John, by the way? I have been more worried than usual about him recently," she asked.

"He seems tired," I replied, "but we have just met him, and have nothing much to go on. He is fine for a while but then suddenly gets exhausted and has to rest. This morning he was up very late, and Fordie seemed concerned."

"You know, Fordie's a wonderful person," Margaret began. "Can you imagine what it must be like living day in and day out with a man as ill as John is, knowing he could die at any moment? Her faithfulness and loyalty are amazing. There's nothing she wouldn't do for him, and she knows him so well that if she's worried there's a reason for it. Her intuition is uncanny. I don't know whether she mentioned it to you, but she is half Romany gypsy. I think that's where she gets all her sensitivity. She keeps quiet about her background, as people are very reserved about such things in this part of the world. But it's a fascinating story. She originally came from a very old English family. Her grandmother lived in a rather grand house in the West Country, I believe. When Fordie's mother was around sixteen, she disappeared. Police searched for weeks. It was written up in the newspapers, and many different theories were put forward. They gave her up for lost in the end, deciding that

79

she must have committed suicide as she had the reputation of being an over-sensitive young girl. Of course, it could never be proved, since they did not find her body. What actually happened was that she had run away with the gypsies.

"Several caravans were parked outside the grounds of the house, and they apparently accepted this young English girl into their circle. She fell in love, traveled with the caravan to France, and Fordie was the result. In fact, Fordie still speaks fluent French, although she doesn't use it very often. Actually, she will probably be quite upset if she knows that I have told you this much. I'm in trouble already so I had better shut up. Cheers!" she said, lifting her glass of beer.

"But how did she come back to England and land up in Wales?" I asked.

"Quite honestly I don't know. She hasn't told John, either, so we remain in the dark. All we do know about Fordie is her kindness and generosity. I also am deeply indebted to her, as she has taught me almost everything I know about the healing herbs that I now use extensively in my own practice. She fits into the play quite perfectly. It's a small world when it comes to this sort of stuff, isn't it?"

"What sort of stuff?" I interrupted. I found a sense of agitation mounting within me. The whole situation, the people, the coming and going, was beginning to feel like a set-up, an unreal one at that.

"Well, you know what I mean," she said laughing. "Fordie is in our lives because we need her. I have joked with her about it many times when I visited her little house, but she just looks at me over the top of her glasses and smiles. I remember a few months ago when we first talked about the imminence of John's death. We were both obviously upset, and although the news was not a surprise it was a shock. Somehow, cancer or no cancer, we all thought he would go on for years. All she said to me at that time was, "Well, dear, a play does not run forever, you know."

"You have both been very lucky to have been introduced to all this," Margaret continued. "Not everyone is, and not many stick it out to the end. You've both learned a little about what it means to be pupils, and that isn't easy in the first place. The only reason that I know anything is because I am hopelessly inquisitive, always on the search and getting myself into deep water, but loving every moment of it! Have another beer—on me this time."

As I got up to get the glasses of beer, I noticed the intensity of Nur's expression as she listened to Margaret speaking. It was as though she was looking for confirmation of some deep intuition of her own. Margaret did not seem offended; in fact, she seemed to understand, for when I came back to the table she had her arm round Nur and they were sitting quietly.

"Don't worry about us," Margaret said to me. "Many of the best things are unspoken."

"You know," she went on, "I am very grateful that you are here with John just now. He is so pleased. He telephoned me the moment he got the letter from Elizabeth that said you were coming. I've lived in this village for years and have watched the change in John. When he was stronger, there was a steady stream of visitors each weekend. People came from the United States who either knew him or had heard of him. Recently, however, he has stopped people from coming. He has often told me that it won't be long before he dies, and he wants to be prepared. Too many visitors would bother him now, as I am sure you understand."

"What exactly was John involved with?" I asked her. "He mentioned that he had worked for the diplomatic service at one time, but I don't know much about the rest of his life."

She smiled, "Many people have asked the same thing." Some pretty amazing people have come to this little village to check up on John, mystics, philosophers, healers of all sorts, and a physicist or two. He wrote a fascinating paper several years ago called "Patterns," which was privately circulated and studied. It concerned a vision he had about an alchemical process that could be used to help sort out the energy crisis. It was all way out of my grasp, but drink up now. We had better get back. You can take me with you if you will as it's raining outside and the walk to John's is a bit far in the wet."

He still seemed very tired when we returned. He was sitting in the dining room with a glass of sherry in his hand, while Fordie bustled about preparing the table for lunch. "You are just in time," said John. "Help yourselves to some sherry from the sideboard if you want."

"Now don't be too long, Mr. John," Fordie announced sharply to him in one ear so that he leaned away from her, laughing. "Lunch will spoil and you know you must eat properly. You'll see he's ready in five minutes, won't you, Mrs. Rhodes? Otherwise everything will be cold."

"See what I mean?" said Margaret. "You can see who rules this house!"

We all laughed then. Nur and I told John about our adventures in the village, and how I had decided that what I really wanted to do was to settle down, while Nur was going to grow herbs and cook delicious meals for the family. "You're an incorrigible romantic," said John. "You would be bored in a week. You can make all the plans you wish, but it all depends on kismet. And we don't want to interfere with that, do we?" he said winking.

During lunch, I noticed Nur looking at Margaret again in that quizzical manner I had seen earlier in the pub. During a lull in the conversation, Nur turned and asked her what she did in the village. "Oh, I do pretty much what everyone does," Margaret answered. "Help with the church, visit old people, watch the world go by, you know what I mean. After all, there isn't much to do here unless you are a hill farmer with sheep to look after. I walk a lot with the dogs, and I try to get away once a year on holiday to Greece—Crete, actually—I love delving into ancient history."

"Now come along, Margaret, I've already told them you're involved with healing," John said. "So why don't you tell them what you really do?"

"It's just that I'm interested in a method of healing called radionics," she said, turning to us, "and although it is a precise science few people accept that yet."

"I've never heard of it. What is it?" I asked.

"It's hard to explain," she replied. "Let's just say that radionics is a science of the future. It is illegal in some countries though it is quite accepted here in England."

"Radionics is an odd word," Nur interrupted. "It sounds as though it uses radio waves or something."

"It's not like that at all, actually. The word is misleading. Some of the instruments do look rather like old-fashioned radio sets, however, and perhaps that's where the name came from, although I don't really know the origin of the word. Basically, it is a sophisticated method of harnessing the power of extrasensory perception to measure imbalances in living organisms. It is a vast subject and my lifetime's interest. However, as I said before, it is very unorthodox and still in its infancy. A few people were had up in court for fraud many years ago, so it is not surprising that radionics is still only discussed among friends or among scientists who are really interested in researching into the subject. You see, the whole principle is exactly contrary to the approach of the normal medical profession, which treats physical symptoms. In contrast, radionics attempts to treat, without the use of drugs, the causes of illness emanating from a formative plane, such as an alteration in the pattern or matrix of a person's etheric substance caused by the crystallization of a shock or opinion fixed in that person's conceptual pattern. This can even come from the unfulfilled wishes of a parent or race as a child's matrix is partly coloured by the imprint or pattern passed on implicitly from his parents. You see, it's important to understand that the uncoloured matrix of a human being contains the fullness of that being's potential in perfection.

"The matrix is like a holographic plate. This perfect matrix, the archetypal idea of the Divine Mother from which creation is continuously becoming, contains in its womb the archetypes of all creatures and kingdoms and however much this perfect matrix is broken into segments of multiplicity in the mind, each individual piece like the hologram still contains within itself the original holistic picture."

The subject was fascinating. John interjected from time to time with some of his own experiences. And I realized later that in the intensity and interest of the conversation I had not noticed the incongruous situation of John, who was so desperately ill, commenting authoritatively on this advanced method of healing.

Throughout the meal, there was a strong pull out of the normal sense of time that I found disquieting. Since my return from Turkey, it had been happening more and more frequently. It was as though more was being packed into a day than was humanly possible. We had barely arrived at John's, yet so much had happened, and the pressure was intense.

Nur remained silent during the time we had been talking, often with that look of agitation on her face. Finally, almost in desperation I think, I asked her what she was looking at. The effect of the question made us all start back. For a moment, Nur's face seemed to change completely. I had a glimpse of the girl with the ball of blue wool I had known in Turkey, whose eyes seemed to see too much. She started shaking slightly. Her knuckles stood out white where she was holding onto the edge of the table. Then quite suddenly she pushed her chair back and ran out of the room.

"What's the matter?" said Margaret, "I hope I have not said anything to offend her. She looked so upset."

"I'll go after her, if you don't mind," I said. "She was ill, but that was a long time ago. I don't understand it."

"Just give her a minute," John said. "She will be all right. Let her calm down, I think I know what has happened."

I told him about the extraordinary circumstances we were involved with at the time we had first met in Turkey. I told John how I had loved Nur even then and that the pressure of the past week had perhaps just been a little too much for her.

"We are all involved with something far greater than we can see or imagine," John said, "and it is sometimes hard to cope, particularly when the pressure is very great."

"Oddly enough," Margaret interjected, "she had the same expression on her face when we were in the pub. I thought that she needed a little comfort, but perhaps it is more than that, John?"

"I believe it is to do with the word *recognition*," John answered. "What I suspect has happened is that Nur has seen something intuitively about the nature of what you are doing. It is as if she is seeing something that she has known before. I do not mean to say that she knew it in a past life or something, but rather that there was a time when she understood these things more easily than she does now, although the result at the time was pretty disastrous. Why don't you go upstairs and find her now?" he said, turning to me.

As I stood up, the door opened and Nur came in, looking the same as ever.

83

I put my arm round her shoulders and led her to her chair.

"Are you all right?" I asked. "What happened?"

"I'm sorry I disturbed your meal," she replied. "It's just that what Margaret was saying had such overwhelming implications that it was suddenly more than I could hold. It was probably because of what happened before."

"Don't worry, my dear," John said. "These things happen, and I expect everything will be made clear when you go round to Margaret's house. By the way, I agree with her. Radionics is a special discipline and will be understood by many people one day, although not in my lifetime, I am afraid."

Just then Fordie came in, pushing a trolley. "Mr. John," she said, "it is time for your rest. You have all been talking too much. I could hear it from the kitchen. Go on with you now."

"She is right—as usual," John said. "I am a bit worn out today. Margaret, dear, would you be very kind and help me change my dressing?"

"May I come too," Nur asked, "so I can learn how to do it next time?"

"It is not very pleasant, I'm afraid," he said, "and really there is no need; but come if you wish."

We helped John upstairs and wheeled his chair so that he could sit by the window. The rain outside had left everything fresh green and sparkling in the afternoon sunlight. Margaret helped John remove his jacket and shirt, and we were immediately hit by the appalling smell of decay. When the dressing was carefully lifted off, the sight of the gaping wound was so shocking I felt I might faint. Nur took my hand. What had once started as a small growth had deteriorated into a deep hollow, eating right into his shoulder. I had had no idea how bad it was. The contrast with the beauty of the countryside shimmering through the windows made it seem worse.

As Margaret prepared the new dressing, John turned to me and smiled gently. "You know, what we *really* are is invisible. If you remember that, you won't worry too much about the wound. Find out who you really are, and you will find that which will never perish. As it is said in the Koran, 'All is perishing except His Face.' As I said before, the great key is to remain conscious at the time of death. This can only happen without fear. It is difficult when you are young and still have your health to contemplate on these things. There is so much living to do, so many dreams to dream, so many things to be accomplished; but, as you grow older, fear starts to creep in. You begin to wonder whether you have lived your life properly; whether you have wasted your time and others'. If you are not careful, you can become so riddled with regrets and guilt that it is impossible not to have fear.

"The Sufis say there are two deadly sins, sloth and fear. Sloth implies a lack of effort in conquering our lower nature and bringing it into order. Procrastinating, presuming that there is someone else to do it for us. Fear comes out of a lack of knowledge and trust.

"Very soon now, the last steps of my life will be completed. The most important thing for me now is to be as awake as I can. Then the real transformation can come that is for all of us if we have worked hard enough during our lifetime. If you are still shocked at a wound, what will it be like for you at the time of death? Seriously, remember what I have said. If you are with me at the right time, it may be possible to experience something of the miracle of transformation, but you must in no way be afraid. This probably sounds a bit dramatic, but there we are." There was tremendous resignation and acceptance in John's voice.

We left him dozing in his chair. I found a new shirt for him hanging in the closet, and Nur had wrapped a blanket round his shoulders.

"Why don't you come round a little later?" Margaret suggested as we climbed down the stairs. "John will probably sleep until six o'clock, and I have a relatively free afternoon."

"We'd love to," Nur replied quickly. "There is so much I would like to ask you about the conversation at lunchtime. I'll tell you what, we'll take a walk and have some fresh air, and then we can meet Margaret afterwards. Does that sound all right?"

"Wonderful!" Margaret replied. "I will have a cup of tea waiting for you."

11

It was quiet by the river. What John had said affected us both very deeply, and we sensed each other's pain. We sat down on a fallen tree where a pool had been cut out in a curve of the river bed. It was so deep that the water looked black. In contrast, the water ran white over the pebbles on the other bank. Here, waterskeeters and caddis flies moved in the quieter back eddies, and once we saw a small eel nosing its way around the edge of the pool looking for food, sometimes standing on its head as it searched under the larger rocks. A fisherman stood further down the river but his dog, a beautiful golden retriever, came bounding up the side opposite barking occasionally. He finally laid down spread-eagled in the shallows opposite, alternatively panting and lapping great gulps of water. We listened as a farm dog barked in the distance, and an occasional car accelerated up the hill towards the village.

"Forgive me for this morning's episode," Nur said finally. "I know it must be hard to understand me sometimes, but it's so difficult finding words to express things that you can see or experience in a totally different dimension. It's as though I go in and out of time. I was always like that, really, but the illness made it more acute, and I've found it difficult to communicate. When I was a little girl, I used to run into the woods when no one understood what I was trying to explain. I could see something no one else could see.

"Since I was tiny, I have been able to sense energy patterns. Everyone used to laugh at me and tell me that I was telling fibs. But it's *true*. There are other worlds right here under our noses and . . . it's all so simple, really."

"But what's that got to do with lunchtime?" I asked her. "Do you think radionics is to do with this as well, then?"

"I don't know, but when I saw Margaret it was like seeing some of the things I experienced all those years ago. That is why I want to go and have a look at what she is doing. All I do know is that Margaret is open to something. It was the same with Elizabeth when I first saw her, and with John. Yet for some reason with John I was not so surprised. You go in and out too, if you see what I mean. Sometimes I can see that you know and that you are on the point of recognition; then you start to doubt, and everything changes back again.

"The formative worlds interpenetrate us all the time. If we were truly opened, it would be possible to see both the formative worlds, within the different dimensions, and the beings who live in these worlds. Does that make sense?"

"But what's happening to *us* in all this, Nur?" I asked. "I keep feeling that I am way out of my depth, and something is going on that is becoming more and more frightening. It is as though we are caught in something beyond our control. We met, and within an incredibly short space of time it became obvious that we were going to be together for a very long time; stranger and stranger things happen to us, and yet we seem to have no say in the matter. If you think about it, this is one of the only times that we have ever had to talk alone!"

"There, you're analyzing it again. Don't doubt. Can you find anything wrong right now? I can't, so that's not so hard to bear is it?"

"Bear what?"

"Oh, for heaven's sake! I know I'm not being very coherent, but you know what I'm trying to say. I'm talking about the two of us and the destiny that brought us together; if we can stand the tension lying within the yearning and the longing to know. Can you stand the inevitability of what will happen? Isn't that why you're getting upset? But since you can't control it, you might as well let it unfold."

"But how can we possibly know what is going to happen?" I asked. "Nobody can know that. There are too many factors to be taken into consideration."

"Oh, please," she begged, sitting up and looking at me intently. "I know it is hard, but you cannot understand any of these things with that mind of yours. We have both got to stop thinking to be able to understand. Can't you see that if this is destined then we have to face everything that is given, whatever comes, whether it is easy or difficult? Don't you see? It's the same with many men. They think too much. And if they do find a woman who will love them and whom they love, they spend the majority of their lives being restless because things do not necessarily work out as they had expected. When the glamour of the meeting dies down, they are too easily fed up with the difficult times; the children, the money, everything."

"Don't be ridiculous," I interrupted. "What on earth is the difference between men and women in this case? Can you honestly tell me that women complain any less than men? This is just plain silly, Nur; what on earth has this got to do with anything at this stage?"

"You just don't understand," she said standing up. "I said that I find it difficult to explain some things, but you are being so thick. I am trying to explain to you that if we just totally agree to be together then everything will work out fine. All these other worlds are there to help us. But men must come to recognize women as they are and for what they contain within them. Can't you see why I was screaming those years ago in Turkey? I was screaming out to be recognized, as I am, the conditioned and the invisible, as John was telling us. We scream out to be recognized as we are. Nothing is going to really change in the world unless this is understood. You will just have another cycle of men and women not coming together, not accepting the unity together, and therefore not accepting all that will be brought to them during their lives. That's why I asked, 'Can we bear it?'—bear what will come and put up with the bad times as well as the good. Well, can we?"

She got up, walked a little way from me, and sat in the shade of an oak tree. Pulling her knees up, she clasped them with her arms and put her head down. It was a picture of despair. Damn! It happened so fast. First we were experiencing everything so deeply together, and then this unbearable sense of separation. I knew that there was something she wanted so much to say. I could sense her pain, her frustration, and her longing, but there was something missing, and I couldn't see it.

We sat by the river in silence, with only the sound of the water running over the rocks. I must have stopped thinking, for quite suddenly I understood. It is said that God made us in his image. If God is perfect, he is also complete in himself. If we are made in his image, then what we really are, the invisible reality of our true selves, it is also complete. If we knew this, we would know ourselves. It is said, "Whoso knoweth himself knoweth his Lord," and thus the cycle would be complete. We alone, in our ignorance, damage the blueprint of our lives and those around us. We alone destroy the living ecology of our land. We alone, in writing our own book, create the concept of good and evil. Yet if we accepted completion, we could participate consciously in unfoldment without interfering with the limitless possibilities that lie within the moment, in essence already complete.

I walked to where Nur was sitting, her back propped against the tree. She smiled. In that silent moment, everything fused and was returned.

At that moment, the dog we had seen on the other side of the river came bounding across the shallows at the end of the pool and ran up the bank toward us. Sensing what was coming, we tried desperately to get up. It was too late! He came straight for us and shook himself violently just where we were sitting—soaking us in a flurry of spray before we could do anything. At that moment, a rabbit hopped out of the wood on our right. With one bound, the dog was after it leaping over us as if we had become invisible.

We doubled up in laughter. "I told you," said Nur, trying to get the words out. "It's a set-up! A wonderful, beautiful, gorgeous set-up. Come on," she said still giggling. "Let's go. We were getting much too serious."

We ran up through the meadow together, the long grass over our ankles, the wind making waves in the spring wheat growing in the field on the other side of the river.

12

Margaret's house lay on the outskirts of the village. Built of stone, it was separated from the road by an old wall covered with creeper. Nine steps led down through a wooden gate to a massive, oak-paneled front door. On the right-hand side was a marvelous bell pull with a notice pinned to the wall behind it, "Please pull gently. This bell is old." We pulled it gently, uncertain of the exact results. But the sound of bells echoed encouragingly inside the house and was closely followed by frenetic barking and Margaret's voice shouting to the dogs to be quiet.

"Come in, come in," she said opening the door. "I am sorry about the animals. They are a bit rude until they get to know you. Come along now," she called to them. Two rather fat yellow Labradors obediently came up, sniffing suspiciously. "They are a little possessive of the house," she said, "but they will be fine in a minute."

Margaret took us into the drawing room, which looked out over the garden at the back of the house. Wide flower borders overflowed in colour along the perfectly kept lawn to a row of fruit trees at the end of the garden. Just outside the window was a rockery, and a small pond in which we could see huge Japanese carp nosing around the lily pads.

"Aren't they beautiful?" she said. "They are my pride and joy. John used to sit there watching the fish for hours. He liked feeding them at sundown. It's sad he cannot get round anymore. We had such wonderful times here. My workshop was downstairs then, but now I have moved my instruments to the attic. I find I can concentrate better if I am a long way away from other people, and I do have so many visitors these days, what with this and that. Actually, we are lucky today. It is a holiday, so my secretary and assistant are away, and if anyone comes I shall just say that they have to come back tomorrow. We'll have some tea now. The kettle is boiling."

While Margaret was getting tea, Nur and I looked at the bookshelves. The walls were lined with books, each section neatly labeled, including ones on all the major religions. Next to them other sections dealt with authors' and poets' commentaries on various aspects of the religion in question. There were endless books on theosophy, the nature of energies, the Druids, Stonehenge, and a particularly intriguing shelf of nothing but ancient Celtic fairytales.

Margaret noticed us when she came in with the tea. "I am afraid I cannot resist buying books," she said. "It is the ideas in the books that fascinate me. I don't have the time to plough through all the text, so I just delve into what the author is trying to put across, and try to sort out the waffle from the essence, if you see what I mean. Books are living creatures," she said. "I try to treat them with all the respect I would the creatures in my garden, or the animals, or humans for that matter—although the latter are more difficult," she said laughing.

After tea, she took us up the narrow flight of stairs to the top floor. In the middle of the landing, there was a hinged ladder that could be pushed back into the roof when it wasn't needed. We climbed carefully, following Margaret, who took the rungs three steps at a time until she disappeared through a hole in the ceiling. "Careful, now," she said. "It's a bit awkward, but it's all right when you get here."

It took a minute to get used to the surroundings. The later afternoon sunlight streamed through a large dormer window at one end of the attic, revealing a room that looked much like a sophisticated electronics laboratory. Instruments lined the shelves, each one a small black box covered in dials. There were various other, more complicated looking machines on the desk in one corner of the room, with several rows of neatly stacked files beside them.

"Well," Margaret began, standing in the middle of the room, "these are some of the radionic instruments we use. It is really impossible to do more than give a very brief outline of the profession, but since you both seemed so interested, I thought that it would do no harm to have a first-hand look."

"All right," said Nur, "but where do we begin? I am not mechanically minded, so I do not know how I am going to understand anything."

"It is not so difficult," answered Margaret. "I am rather like you. I do not get on with ordinary science very well but rely on faculties other than rational deduction to understand things. As I said before, it all has to do with extrasensory perception. Because we are not dealing with a three-dimensional physical body, but with the etheric substance we are not limited by time or distance in the normal sense of those words but can treat a patient anywhere in the world, even if we have not met him or her personally. It is different from everyday life, because we are involved with the matrix, or blueprint of physical and emotional bodies."

"But what do all these instruments do?" I asked her.

"In one sense, they don't do anything," she replied. "In another, they are entirely dependent on the operator. Let us just say that they are really a rather subtle form of computer. With the aid of the instruments, we can measure imperfections in the force field that precipitate illness and disease, and with that information it is possible to discover a pattern or frequency that can treat the imperfection. The theory is that if we can treat the formative world the physical one will come back into alignment and balance quite easily."

Nur was examining one of the instruments carefully.

"You know," she said finally, "I can almost see the emanations coming out of this box. It is amazing—or am I dreaming?"

"No, there are some people who can sense such things," Margaret answered.

"The emanations you are observing, Nur, are dependent on the rates of vibration coming from the pattern set up on the instruments. It is rather like smoke which is an emanation from a burning fire which is vibrating at a very high rate indeed. I am not sensitive to these things myself, but for some it is too much even to come into the room. Different patterns are continuously being set up and broadcast to patients all over the world. Each instrument here is treating someone at this very moment."

"It's too way out for me," I said laughing.

"No it isn't!" said Nur with some irritation. "I think I can see what Margaret is doing, and so can you if you stop trying to understand with the mind. It is what I thought it would be. When I was in that mad state, I could see patterns everywhere. If someone was angry, it was one type of pattern; if someone was sick, it would be another. It wasn't just the colors of the aura that I could see, but the subtlety of the patterns within the colors and even *before* color. Radionics is something like touching up a negative to get a good photograph, isn't it, Margaret?"

"You could certainly look at it that way. Of course, some people do not need instruments at all to achieve the same results. I know of several famous healers who do the same thing; the only difference is that we can treat many people simultaneously once we have the necessary data at our disposal. But it *is* like working with a negative."

"Look," Nur said, tugging at my sleeve, "this is really important. It has to do with what we were talking about at breakfast, treating the cause and not the symptoms, which is real healing. If it hadn't been for people who understood these things and who could work with the portion of my mind that was shattered, I could have been locked up and given something terrible like shock treatment. It's wonderful, isn't it?" she said to me. Without waiting for an answer, she repeated, "It is wonderful because a whole new world opens up for us."

"All right, then," I said, surprised to find myself feeling defensive, "but what about John?" I asked Margaret, "Couldn't you do anything for him?"

"I thought someone would ask that," she replied. "But to answer your question, there is no cure-all. No doctor in the world can guarantee the treatment he or she is giving. *In radionics or in any form of therapy work can be done only to a certain level.* In John's case, it might well have been possible to do something, but by the time the cancer was firmly established in his physical body, he just did not seem to respond." She paused for a moment. "Anyway, sometimes it is just not right for someone to get better. There are other, higher reasons for this, and we must always remember that appearances are not everything. Perhaps that is something to understand in the tragedy of John's illness.

"Come on now," she said, putting her arms round us. "It is time for you to get back. I cannot come round this evening, and I do not know whether Fordie is coming to help with John's supper. I am sure you can get him something, anyway. Give him my love, won't you?"

13

It was getting dark as we got back to John's house. Nur talked excitedly all the way, but I was tired and still very tense from the meeting with Margaret. John was waiting for us. He looked refreshed from his rest and seemed eager to talk. This time, I felt I just could not cope with any more and asked if I could be excused to rest before supper. He smiled at me. "Where is your stamina?" he asked. I took a deep breath to try to answer, but he went right on: "Don't worry, I understand. Nur and I can enjoy ourselves together, can't we?" he said holding her hand. "Come down when you are rested, and we will see what is coming up."

When I finally woke, it was dark. Looking at my watch, I realized that I had missed supper, so I lay back in bed for a while and tried to sort out the experiences and thoughts of the day into some coherent pattern. Time had become so condensed these past few days that it was becoming increasingly difficult to keep up with what was going on. Certainly this period was like no other I could remember. The sense of inevitability and the internal pressure arising as more and more new ideas were fed to us made any distinctions in time seem completely arbitrary.

In particular, I found the imminence of John's death subtly changing my own attitude to life. Looking back, I realized that when I was sent back from Turkey to meet Elizabeth something had been set in motion in my life that was culminating in John's death. It was the inevitability that was the mystery. The set-up, as Nur called it. A mystery, that in some strange way the map of our lives is already set in its completion in the matrix, but that it is up to us to fulfill the possibilities. If we accept this, it seemed we could know where to be and what to do. Yet it occurred to me then that the real mystery hidden in all this was that it is not possible to know what to do in advance. Action is taken in the ever-present unfolding of the one moment. I saw just how often I had stopped the natural flow in my own life simply by imposing my own opinions on a situation rather than seeing the moment, and the situation arising from the moment, as the teaching that was necessary.

As I lay back in bed, listening to John and Nur speaking in the room below, I found myself going in and out of the two sorts of time that had now become quite real to me. At one moment I was in the world of passing time as we normally see and identify it. I followed the pictures and images passing by the screen of my mind, just as I might observe the traffic passing in the street outside the window, or the different events of the day, one following another. Then I was in another time in which everything was complete at once. Time stopped still and all the events that before seemed sequential, were made real precisely through their movements in passing time. Everything was contained in one moment; all the events of the day were seen in one picture. In the next instant, I saw again only the events themselves as they occurred sequentially in time.

It was, in many ways, an unnerving experience. I knew that the mind could only understand a fraction of truth, and that I would have to find a way to see passing time objectively without becoming locked into it by the senses. Yet, at that moment, life took on a new meaning for me. I cannot say that it made it any easier, but that was not the point. What it did was to show me the shallowness of routine life in which I had considered that I had some right to understand with the mind as it was, not realizing that only through the sacrifice of our own linear thinking we can begin to comprehend who we really are and what our purpose in life is.

Nur and John were talking happily when I came downstairs. "What on earth have you been doing?" asked Nur. "You've missed supper, a wonderful conversation, and a bottle of wine. That is very unlike you," she said laughing.

"Don't push him too far," John said. "He is only half awake as it is. There is supper in the oven and a salad in the fridge if you wish."

"I'm not actually hungry," I said. "I have been lying awake in bed for quite a long time contemplating what has been happening. I feel so full already I don't need any food, thank you."

"So what have you been contemplating, if you will pardon my asking? There isn't much time, and I want to know what you are getting out of all these experiences. Nur tells me that you both had a good time with Margaret."

"A lot of that was way over my head, John. Nur seems to understand it better than I do. There have been many realizations, and I suppose it will take ages for me to get them down into some sort of coherent whole, but what has come through most clearly is to do with the nature of time." I explained as best I could what I had seen of passing and eternal time. John nodded in agreement and sat back in his chair puffing his pipe.

"Yes," he said, "the cross is a good symbol to describe those two aspects of time. The vertical bar of the cross represents the eternal aspect of time, and the horizontal bar the aspect of passing time. Where the two bars cross, it is possible to see both times at *once*. The flashes of deep understanding we have come from that point. But there is something else to consider. When we do not first accept things as they are, we are almost bound to want to change them by imposing our concept on perfection. We are working from our own selfish desires, from our egos. In a sense, we create another sort of time, imposed on that which is already perfect in essence. It is not difficult to understand, but, like everything else, until someone comes along to tell us this it is difficult to accept."

"Curiously enough, John, that was one of the things that I was considering upstairs just a few minutes ago," I interjected. "It is similar to imposing opinions on a play before it is acted out."

"That's right. In the process of imposing these opinions, to use your expression, we build up all sorts of karma for ourselves and for others. We are forced to play out what we have created in the mind, and we are forced to pay for our stupidity and ignorance by playing a role in the book that we ourselves have written. It's quite frightening to realize this, but it is most certainly a step towards real freedom. If you understand some of these things, you won't cause yourselves so much pain, and so you can help others to understand.

"I know this is a lot to stomach all at once, but I want to put it to you another way. Let us, all of us, look at what is going on in the room at this moment. On the one hand, we can see that everything here depends on what has happened before. For example, if you had not, on some level, searched for a partner with whom you could share your spiritual journey, it is unlikely that you and Nur would be sitting here with me. Equally, if she had not come to certain realizations we could not be talking as we are, for I can only really tell you what you already know. For my part, I, too, had wished and prayed that someone would come along with whom I could share these things before I died.

"On the other hand, there is another way of seeing things that is equally correct, and that is to attempt to live life without imposing anything on it whatsoever. One begins to feel that everything was set before the world of passing time as we see it and that we are merely actors fulfilling our role in the completion of the act. The play is really *As You Like It!*

"That is what I am attempting to do now—to play out what is in the moment and not to impose my concepts on it. If you both do the same, you will not be working with 'false time,' but will be accepting things as they are and thus accepting the possibility that they will unfold in perfection.

"If we stop for a moment, it is possible to perceive a pattern in our lives; the motivators that have influenced us become more obvious. We are able to see life unfolding from *both ends at once*, coming into the present moment. But until we have got to a certain point of realization, this is not possible, because everything is still seen as a series of apparent causes and effects."

John smiled and lit his pipe again. Nur was sitting by his feet. She had an unforgettable expression on her face. She seemed to be in a world of total gentleness, perhaps hearing and seeing things that she had always known. At least, that was the way I experienced it. The room was still. She turned to me for a moment, and our eyes met. There was an unspoken bond of recognition, which a long time afterwards, I too came to understand.

John smiled. He looked suddenly tired. "Would you like to rest now?" I asked him. "It is getting quite late."

"No, we have so little time, and as long as I can keep going and as long as you are listening, it is important to continue. You see, the understanding of time brings us closer to the possibility of going beyond. I will be all right. Why don't you get me a whisky and soda?"

"I'll go," said Nur. "How do you like it?"

"Whichever way you make it for me," he answered. "These vices do not matter much anymore, and a stiff drink sometimes helps the pain."

I had completely forgotten! The shock of realization carried me back to childhood and the anguish of being scolded for forgetting everyone else but myself. John sensed immediately what was in my mind, for he turned to me, and spoke with great command and tenderness. "Don't be sentimental about my discomfort, for sentimentality can be the greatest enemy of love. I want you to listen and to understand, not to get immersed in fear and guilt. The pain I have is mine; it is not yours. You have your own to deal with, whether physical or emotional. You cannot help me with the pain anymore than the doctors can. You can be sympathetic, but please don't identify. Never identify yourself with anything, not your own so-called problems nor those of another. Be yourself at all times. Keep your mind on what you are doing outwardly or inwardly, so you may continue on the path of service."

I was sitting next to him. There were tears in my eyes, but they were more from gratitude than from personal pain. Nur came back with drinks for us all. I saw her look at me, but she said nothing.

"Now, then," John said, "let us take our conversation a bit further. Listen carefully. As we gather ourselves more completely in the present, the fear of death dissolves and the point of conception moves closer. So-called death and conception are actually in the same moment. Something gives way, makes space, if you like, for something else. A certain energy is released in dying, and that energy gives life to something that wishes to come into manifestation."

"Can you say, then, what you mean by 'conception'?" asked Nur. "Do you mean the literal conception of a child?"

"Come, now," he said. "Remember, you are invisible. The physical form is just the vehicle. Conception takes place in a world before time, and then, little by little, the form is built to contain that which is really coming into manifestation. What is seen in this world is merely the physical expression of other, greater worlds, manifesting here, interpenetrating this world.

"At the moment of a person's death, a child is conceived. It may not be just a physical child. Think of the world of ideas and that the quality of what is born depends at least partly on the parents' degree of consciousness. The energy released at the time of death, if used properly, can help bring about the birth of an idea in a real way. If a man or a woman dies consciously, the effect of this act is so great that it is literally impossible for anyone witnessing the event not to be changed. To die consciously means not only to be totally awake, but also to have nothing left in this world to hang onto; no anger, resentment, fear, and so on. Nothing is left but the knowledge of Love itself. Do you understand, Nur? Can you see what I am trying to transmit? What does this mean? Obviously, it is impossible to say more than just a little about this. The inner experience must be your own, not mine. So take what I have said for now, and when the time is right perhaps you will be able to see what I am trying to express."

"What about reincarnation?" I asked. "How does that fit into the ideas you were expressing?"

He looked a little weary, and I wondered if I had asked the wrong question. "I am bound to try to answer you, but I am going to take the liberty of asking a question first. If there is such a thing as reincarnation, could you tell me what it is that reincarnates?"

He leaned back in his chair and looked at me intently. Nur was still sitting quietly. She had not looked up when he asked the question.

"I suppose it is the soul that takes on another body," I answered.

"Good," John said, "but do you know what the soul is or are you quoting others? Because if you can tell me what the soul is, then the very question of reincarnation will simply not exist. It is only because you do not know that you ask this question."

"Look," Nur interrupted. "We have got to stop theorizing. Reincarnation is a theory that some people from certain traditions believe in. What John is talking about is not theory. I know it isn't!"

John smiled and turned to me again. "In one sense, there is reincarnation," he continued, "but only if we still live in a world of sequential time in which life starts with conception and birth and goes on through adolescence and puberty to old age and death. In that world, there can be said to be memory patterns that we see as our past lives or the past lives of others. Through this belief system, we can explain away a lot of things, such as synchronicity or *déjà vu* experiences. However, when we say '*our*' past lives or, more particularly, when someone says '*my*' past life we rarely stop to consider *who* is saying '*my*' or '*our*.' Look at it this way: If we do not have a permanent 'I', a different 'I' is speaking in each moment. Now, this can give rise to some confusion, particularly when two people are attempting to communicate.

"The mind will try to discard what I am saying. That is why you are feeling resistance. But if you consider it, you will see that when people discuss reincarnation, they seldom speak from their eternal nature, but speak rather from a relative part of themselves."

"But John," I asked, "what about the Oriental religions that affirm reincarnation. Are you saying that they are wrong?"

"I have not even said that I *don't* believe in reincarnation. I am merely asking you to look carefully into its true nature. I can say, although I know it sounds infuriating, that, yes, there is reincarnation and, no, there is not.

"Look, both of you. I am asking this most sincerely, because I have no doubt we were brought together for a reason—you cannot understand without sacrificing something. You must give up your *concept* of reincarnation. It is the conceptual mind that gets us into trouble and that keeps trying to repeat itself and to prove its own existence separate from unity. Perhaps we could be quiet for a while and could let all this sink in."

He leaned back in his chair and closed his eyes. I held Nur's hand. Little by little, my mind grew still. Sensory feelings calmed, and I could feel that John was working with me in a very deep and personal way. All that remained was the movement of breath, which seemed to emerge from exactly that one point of fusion in eternal and passing time. In that point, there was no repeating of anything. Everything was in one moment, forever and in all ways. The question we had been discussing contained its own answer. Hours passed, or so it seemed, but when we eventually opened our eyes we saw that less than five minutes had elapsed.

John was asleep. We decided not to wake him and covered him gently with a blanket. We put more logs on the fire and turned down the lights. The flames made incredible patterns on the walls and ceiling distorting our shadows in the half-light. The moon, which was nearly full, lit the dew in the meadow turning the grass silver green. The river shimmered in the moonlight. It was very still. We did not speak again as we went upstairs to our room, and the timeless moment remained.

14

Just after dawn, I heard John moving downstairs. It had been impossible to sleep, and I was still restless. When I went to see if John needed help, I found him in much the same state. His usual gentleness and humour were gone, and he was fussing over the slightest thing. I woke Nur, and between us we changed the dressing on his wound, which looked somehow deeper and more livid. John complained of the pain and seemed fed up with it all. Finally he asked to be left alone until Fordie had prepared breakfast. We propped him up with cushions and left him sitting by the window with a cup of coffee.

"What's wrong?" Nur asked as we walked slowly down to the riverbank. "You and John seemed upset this morning."

I shrugged. "I'm just nervous," I answered. "And it is obvious that John is going through something."

"Well, I feel fine," she replied. "After all, this is only the third morning we have been here so it's not surprising you feel odd with all that has happened. I thought we had been here for weeks until I looked at my diary this morning. It's crazy."

"Has it only been three days?" I asked. "What on earth will it be like if the rest of our time together is as intense as the last few days have been? I don't know if I could take it."

"Well, we're going to have to try. Both of us know the inevitability of John's death, and I know he wants us with him. It probably seems difficult because we are hardly used to him yet. In a way, it is as though we haven't really met. There has been no time for informalities—just more and more teaching. I would love to ask him about his life, but I get the feeling that it is not the time. It seems all we are to do is to remain completely open and serve him as best we can. Whatever feelings I have had about his death I have simply put out of my mind so that I don't dwell on them."

"I wish I could say the same," I replied. "I just can't get used to the imminence of John's death. I have witnessed death before, but it was somehow different, because they were all surprises. There wasn't this awful sense of waiting."

The smell of fresh mushrooms being grilled wafted down the pathway as we got back to the house. Fordie's bicycle, with its old-fashioned handlebars, was propped up against the gate, and there were fresh flowers from her garden still sitting in the wicker basket that was strapped on behind the seat. John was sitting at the head of the table immersed in a newspaper.

"Ah," he said looking up. "Did you have a good time? I had a wonderful two hours to myself in which I got a few inner things done as well as writing some long overdue letters. You know, we are only free to go on when we have completed a project or decision. However, your breakfast is getting cold, so help yourself to what you want from the sideboard; Fordie has everything ready."

The tension we had felt passed, and we spent a wonderful hour going over the things that John had told us, clearing up much of the confusion that I had experienced. John seemed extraordinarily happy, and eventually I asked him to explain.

"Well, these things happen," he said. "You know that. Sometimes you can put your finger on the cause, and sometimes you can't. Many's the time that I have been through similar experiences, only to find later that there has been some tragedy in the world, a plane crash, an earthquake. Something has happened or is about to happen, but this time I am not sure. I feel better now, but if I am completely honest, I can still pick up on something. What about you?" he asked abruptly.

The telephone rang noisily. It gave my nerves a tremendous shock after what John had been saying. I heard Fordie moved down the passage to answer it. There was silence for a moment, and then I heard her talking rapidly in French. Her voice was agitated, and the conversation went on for a while. Everything was quiet over the table. John did not seem to take much notice and had immersed himself again in his newspaper. Nur and I looked at each other in the mutual understanding we were beginning to share. We heard the click of the receiver and Fordie's steps going back to the kitchen. John's newspaper rustled as he turned a page. The atmosphere was electric.

Nur and I cleared the dishes together and took them back to the kitchen to find Fordie. She was looking out of the window by the sink when we came in and it was obvious that she was deeply upset. "It's all right," she said as Nur went to comfort her, "but I must speak to you privately, if you please." We sat down on the back porch together.

"I have just had a call from France," Fordie began. "One of my relatives is desperately ill and has summoned the family. I am the last one and I must go.

I have no alternative, as I come from a gypsy background and our ways are very clear. But last night I lay awake, and I used some of the old methods to see if I could find out what was in the wind. Mr. John is very close now. I knew it anyway, but now I don't have much doubt, and although he seems to be better and has plenty of strength, I don't think it will be long—perhaps no more than three days. I would do anything for Mr. John," she said. "I never expected to leave when he needed help." Her voice was full and it was difficult to speak. "I must say, it's a funny way to end the time together."

"Don't worry, Fordie," Nur said, "we'll look after him; you know that. There's Margaret to help, and you may not be right. You could come straight back then, after you've done what you have to do in France."

She shook her head, "I am right," she said, "and I want you to get Miss Elizabeth. I promised her that if anything happened I would telephone her." She closed her eyes and breathed deeply, collecting herself. When she spoke again, her voice was clear and practical. "You'll have to take things on now. The most immediate thing is the shopping. There's a meat pie today, and fish for tomorrow's dinner, which has yet to be collected from the van by the post office. You'll have to get in all the rest of the weekly supplies as well. I have to go quickly, so I'll get the train to Southampton where I can get a ferry. By the way, in Mr. John's bathroom cupboard there is a box of tablets marked with his name. They are for emergencies only."

"Can't I take you when I go to get Elizabeth?" I asked her.

"Thank you, but John will need you here today when he hears the news. I'll leave the address pinned on the board by the kitchen window so you can't lose it. You will let me know if anything happens, won't you? I'll go and tell Mr. John now. Perhaps you could stay here and help with the dishes."

She came out of John's study some time later, collected her things in the kitchen, and walked down the pathway to pick up her bicycle by the gate. She turned back once to wave to John. We were standing in the doorway behind him and waved goodbye to her together.

"So," he said, turning his chair round, "that was a surprise! Never mind, it is quite right that Fordie has to go. The Romanies are a proud race and they have strict codes. It is necessary that she be with her family."

"Fordie told you to call Elizabeth, didn't she?" he asked. "I don't want to bother her, and I am sure we can manage all right between us." Nur and I caught each other's eyes for a brief moment. John must have noticed, as he questioned us disbelievingly. "Surely you've called Elizabeth since you left London to say you'd arrived safely . . . haven't you?" It was almost unbelievable, but in all that had happened in the last three days we had completely forgotten to call Elizabeth! I guessed that John had realized this but was just waiting for the right time to say something.

103

"You have called her, haven't you?" he asked again. "Because if you haven't, then you both still have a very great deal to learn. After all, she is the link in the chain for you just now. What sort of manners are these? I'm not going to say anymore. It takes too much time and energy, and we have better things to talk about. But I suggest you call her now, and when you have finished please come back and see me." He turned his chair round with a quiet finality to face out across the garden.

Nur and I went back into the kitchen to finish the clearing up. If it hadn't been for the intensity of the situation, we would have had a very difficult scene. Both of us were on the verge of blaming the other for forgetting to call Elizabeth, and the guilt we both felt magnified the incident. It was Nur who saved the situation. "All right, we both forgot. I am ashamed of myself, but let's leave it now and call Elizabeth with Fordie's message."

We tried several times to get through, but the line was always busy, so much so that we had it checked by the operator. It was so seldom that Elizabeth spoke on the telephone, and we wondered if the line was out of order. Finally, we got a ringing tone on the other end. "Yes, this is Elizabeth," she said, "Who is that?"

Nur had dialed the number, and I was on an extension upstairs so we could both speak to her. "Good heavens," Elizabeth said. "What happened to you? You might as well have disappeared off the face of the earth. In fact, I was just about to call and see if you were still alive. Now then," she said in her usual brusque tone, "what is it?"

"Well, first of all," I answered, "we both wanted to apologize for not calling sooner. To be quite frank, time has gone haywire, and it was only this morning that we realized that we had already been here three days. It might as well have been ten years as half a day."

"Tut! Tut! Time may seem odd when you stop thinking with the mind, but that is no excuse for not having manners. But enough of that, I think you've got a message, haven't you?"

Little by little, we went on to explain what had been happening and the experiences we had been through, leading up to Fordie's announcement a short time ago. Elizabeth was silent on the other end.

"You see, Fordie felt that I should drive down to pick you up," I said, "but John says that we can manage. What are we to do?"

"Take no notice of John," replied Elizabeth. "Of course I should be there. You say you have things to do today, so I shall expect you in time for breakfast tomorrow. It won't take you more than four hours at that time of the morning. If you leave very early, you can be here around nine o'clock. In the meantime, if anything happens, you are to call me. Do you understand? And don't be so asleep in the future—you might forget where you're going!" Just

104

before the telephone was put down I heard that deep rumbling sound from the other end. Elizabeth was laughing to herself.

We told John that Elizabeth had insisted she wanted to come. He smiled then and seemed relieved. "All right," he said, "but I don't want any dramas. I'm feeling fine, so why don't you go out shopping as you said you would? Then you could get back here for lunch. I've a lot of letters still to write, which will keep me busy. Just leave some coffee and biscuits, and I'll be fine."

By the time we reached the village shop, the news that Fordie was leaving had traveled ahead of us. "How will you manage?" the shopkeeper asked. "If you need any help, you just call me and I'll come down and cook. My husband is out all day, and the daughter can mind the shop. Is Mr. John all right?"

We reassured her that everything was fine, but there was a look on her face that made me think that perhaps Fordie had said something about her premonition. We bought all the necessary provisions, and she added another of the cheeses that John liked so much. "Don't forget, now," she said as we left, "call me and I'll be there in a few minutes if you need help."

We took a small lane on our return to the house. Nur had said that she needed some fresh air, and there was plenty of time before lunch. It was a beautiful day. The hedges were dusted with green buds that were just about to burst into leaf. Crocuses and daffodils blossomed in the gardens of the cottages that we passed. The hills were speckled white with newly born lambs, and blossoms were just starting to show pink-white on the trees. We stopped and walked through a wood that seemed alive with birdsong; the watery call of the thrush, the trill of the warblers, and the plaintive cry of the robin. We heard the first cuckoo. Nur did not speak, and we walked silently, hand in hand. The sense of emergency we'd been experiencing seemed foreign and out of place here.

At the far end of the wood, there was a view over the valley beyond where we could just see a small chapel standing alone, less than a mile away. "Look," Nur said, "let's walk to it. I'd like to sit there for John." She climbed over the gate marking the boundary of the wood and started running through the field ahead of us. "Wait!" I called.

We collapsed on an oak bench outside of the chapel grounds, completely out of breath. A stream ran just beside the lane leading up to the chapel, which was shaded by an extraordinary yew tree that must have been several hundred years old. Apart from the gentle trickle of the stream and the liquid notes of a wren calling from the hedgerow, there was no sound at all.

Nur and I walked quietly through the graveyard behind the church, looking at the stones. Some dated from the early seventeenth century, but moss and lichen had grown over many, obliterating the names and dates of the persons who were buried there by the passage of centuries. The grounds were beautifully kept, and there were fresh flowers on some of the newer graves.

The chapel was entered through a covered porch surmounted by Gothic arches made of huge oak timbers. There were notices pinned on a board in front of the door and underneath was a small offertory box towards the upkeep of the building. One of the notices described the history of the chapel, which dated back to the twelfth century, and told the story of a monk who had lived in a hut behind the present site, where there was a sacred well. The waters were holy; people from all over Wales had come to drink it and carry it back for the sick.

"This place reminds me of the chapel at Ephesus," Nur said. "It's got the same feeling of peace and stillness, and I can sense the hundreds of pilgrims who have come here over the centuries. Look, I hadn't noticed before, it's dedicated to Mary," she said, pointing to the sign above the door. "I feel like I'm in two places at once. Do you feel it?"

It was true. There was an extraordinary sense of completion present, the sense of woman complete, as represented by the Virgin Mary, the perfect matrix. I took Nur's hand once we entered the chapel.

Inside it was perfectly plain; whitewashed walls, rough oak benches, and an altar with a simple brass cross. Nothing distracted from the perfection of the design of the building and the gentle grace that swept through us. Nur walked quietly to the front and knelt by the altar rails. I sat on a bench where we had been standing. My mind wandered back over my own life, watching scenes unfold in the deepening silence. I saw myself as a child, playing in the woods and the open fields. I remembered how free I felt then. I looked back over the days of city life when I had been a stockbroker, and then a hard-bitten advertising executive until something had awakened me and I had started on the long search for some meaning in life. There was a journey round the world, seeking, looking for answers in Japan, in the ashrams in India, in the northern Himalayas above Pakistan until the day I had met my teacher in an antique shop in London, which led me to Turkey and the world of the dervishes. It seemed almost incongruous in this tiny church. It was as though I had returned to the point where the journey started—or else I had never left. Memories flooded in, and I allowed myself to be drawn into all the sensations that we experience—joy, sadness, bitterness and grief. I prayed that the memories would be dissolved and that only what was useful would remain as part of the pattern of my life.

I don't know whether I actually went to sleep, but I lost all sense of time. It was Nur who brought me back.

"Look at the time! We have been here for ages. We're going to be terribly late. "Let's take some water back for John."

The well had a low stonewall around it and someone had left glass bottles beside it. We filled one and ran back across the fields to the car.

"Oh, I hope it's all right. I don't know what happened to us. Quick—let's go," she said.

I thought you were never coming back," John said as we came through the door of the house, our arms piled high with groceries. "You said you were only going out for the shopping, and it's been hours."

He looked drawn again, but there was no sense of anger in his voice. "What have you been doing?"

"I'm sorry, John," I said. "It was my fault. Time seemed to slip by. We went for a walk and stopped at an old church. It won't take long to get your lunch. Really, I'm very sorry."

"Don't worry," he said. "I'm not hungry but my dressing needs changing now."

I realized he was in pain, and it was the first time that I had seen him in such a state. We had been so stupid to forget his needs so easily! We helped him upstairs to his room and Nur got the dressings from the bathroom closet. John did not speak and seemed to be sinking rapidly into a semi-conscious state. "Quick—help me!" Nur exclaimed as he started to fall forward out of the chair. He was a dead weight, and it took all my strength to hold him. "Shall we get the doctor?" I asked him, but there was no answer.

"John," I said leaning down close to his ear," John, can you hear me?" Again there was no answer. By now he was half slumped against the chair. "Ring the doctor quickly, Nur, I'll try to move him."

"No, we'd better not touch him till we get some advice. Let's just cover him with a blanket. I'll hurry." Her voice was tense with concern.

She ran down the stairs, and I heard her talking to the doctor and the sound of her feet running back up the stairs into the bathroom. She returned with the box of tablets Fordie had told us about. John was still slumped in his chair, his face chalky grey. "Hurry," I said to Nur. "See if you can get one of them into his mouth." It was impossible. His teeth were clenched tightly. Finally Nur crushed the tablet and managed to get most of the powder inside his lips. "Oh God, is he dying?" Nur cried. "Help me, let's try to massage his chest." There was no reaction. His breathing was very slow, and there was a rasping sound in his chest. We still had not had time to put on the new dressing, and we were both panicked, not knowing what to do.

There was the sound of gravel crunching on the drive just then. Nur moved quickly to the door, but there was no need. The doctor hurriedly opened the front door and ran past her up the stairs into John's room. Without a word, he opened his bag, took out a syringe, and pulled back John's shirt. "Let's pray we're in time," he said. "Tell me exactly what happened."

We explained that we had stayed out longer than we had intended, that John was upset and in pain when we got back, and that this had happened soon afterwards.

The doctor finished the injection, took John's blood pressure, and then massaged his chest some more. "It looks as though John's had a minor stroke," he said finally. "He made me promise never to take him to the hospital. It makes things difficult, but if necessary I can get oxygen sent round."

Just then, I noticed a slight movement in John's eyes. Very slowly, and with great effort, he opened them as we moved his head back into an upright position. The colour began to come back into his face. The doctor gave him a second injection and forced another tablet into his mouth. "Please go downstairs," he said. "I want to be alone with him for a while. I'll call if I need you."

We sat on the stone steps outside the front door. Neither of us could speak. I heard the deep tick of the grandfather clock in the hall and the muffled sound of voices from upstairs.

The doctor joined us a short time later. "Don't worry," he said, "he'll be all right—at least for now. We were just in time; another few minutes, and he would have been gone. I must go and wash now, and then there are a few things I want to talk to you about. You needn't go upstairs just yet, I have given him a heavy sedative, and it is better that he sleep."

"I should introduce myself," he said when he returned a little later. "My name is Jim Butler. John has just been speaking to me about you. Presumably you know of his condition? We do not know how long he has, but he has probably told you this. All of us have been amazed by his lack of fear. He has recently taken myself and Margaret Rhodes as his confidants in this and asked that old acquaintances do not visit him. He said that he had got his life in order, yet there was something else he had to do before he died. We used to ask him what it was but he would not say, or perhaps could not. He just repeated that he felt there was still time to complete something. After all these years, I still don't know what he's getting at most of the time. Even with the scientists who used to visit him I was completely out of my depth. But he has told me that you two came to help toward this completion. Does that make sense to you?"

"Not really," I answered. "All we feel is that we are playing roles in a play with an inevitable ending. It's as though we're caught in something we can't

108

get out of even if we wanted to. John seems like my own father in a strange way."

"I understand; he has meant a great deal to all of us in the village. He is an extraordinary man, continuously giving, never speaking ill of anyone and seldom complaining, although he is in immense pain most of the time. His courage and bravery are an example to us all. I won't ask you how you came to be involved with him, as I must be going on my rounds, but perhaps we will have time to meet sometime. If you get the chance, you could come round and have a glass of sherry with my wife and I. I know she would be pleased to meet you.

"Now, then, John should sleep for a couple of hours. When he wakes up, give him the tablets I left on his bedside table. There are three of them. If he doesn't want to take them, then insist. He'll probably listen to you even if he won't to me!"

We took turns sitting with John while he slept. The drugs had worked, and, apart from an occasional movement of his arm, he did not stir. Jim had somehow or other got him on to the bed and had changed his dressing. He was resting peacefully. It was nearly sunset when we saw him open his eyes. Nur was holding his hand. "It's all right now, John," she said. "The doctor says that you are going to be fine." He smiled as I handed him the tablets. "Dear old Jim," he said. "He worries too much. I've had these attacks before, you know. I hate these damn pills, they make me feel drowsy. Keep them for another day," he said brushing my hand away.

"Now, John," said Nur firmly. "*Please*. Jim said that you have had a minor stroke and that you really must take them. Anyway, these are not the same as the other ones. These are not to put you to sleep; they are to wake you up."

Finally we persuaded him to take them, but then he wanted to come downstairs! His recovery was remarkable; it was almost unbelievable to see him so changed.

"Wouldn't it be better if you stayed up here and rested?" We begged but he wouldn't take any notice. "This is *my* life," he said. "Come on, now!"

We helped him into his chair and took him down to the sitting room. The long shadows on the lawn stretched towards the windows. "We've got a lot to be grateful for, you know. Let's be quiet for a while together."

We sat with him in silence. His eyes were closed, but he was not sleeping. Occasionally he leant over and touched one of us in a gesture of reassurance. We had come to love him unconditionally, and this made the pain and fear that we were both experiencing easier to bear. Years later, we were able to talk about this, but at the time it was more a question of being present for all that was happening in the moment and for the loving kindness and generosity that flowed through him.

There is no way that I could describe the experience I felt during that time. We were together in complete peace and freedom. The experiences of the world as I knew it disappeared; there was only a deep inner sense of the rightness of things. Everything was in its proper place. I understood the nature of false time and how it had tyrannized me in the past, bringing in so much fear, fear of living, fear of loss, fear of not succeeding, fear known and unknown. I could see the pointlessness of it and the pointlessness of the fear of death. In those moments, there was no death. Everything was as it is, *at once,* for there is Only One, and only one moment of creation. Everything was contained in that moment, as the whole of a symphony is contained in the first note. Life, our lives, were all contained in the Divine Breath blowing across the world, bringing with it the vast miracle of diversity, the unique expression of humanity, the changing seasons, the warmth of sunlight, and the scent of roses. Personal identity vanished in the Unity, swallowed up by an experience of One Essential Reality. In the beginning was the Word, and the Word was with God. Christ said, "I am with you even unto the end of time." In the world beyond time, beyond experience, the knowledge of Unity remains.

I knew, then, that I had been dead and now I was alive. The illusions of death had gone, and the realization that we are all dead until we wake came in such a flash of recognition that the energy of release coursed through every part of me. So powerful was the experience that my body began to tremble. I felt John's hand on my arm. "Do not worry," he said. "The body will look after itself. Just let it be transformed. Remain the observer, and there will be no danger." I knew unconditional love, that indeed I was loved as we all are loved, for surely Love is the cause of Creation.

We sat quietly together. The sun had gone down and the only light came from the flickering embers in the fireplace.

It was still dark when I left the next morning. Nur made coffee and awakened me very early. "We must be quiet," she said. "John is still asleep. He needs to get all the rest he can. Come back soon—it will be harder without you here." By the gate, we held each other. "It will only be about twenty-four hours. Don't worry." I watched her as she walked back into the house. The light on the porch silhouetted her for a moment, and then the door closed.

On the drive to London, I found myself increasingly edgy. I felt as if I were racing time, yet I knew that this was not so. Part of me still lived in the world of apparent cause and effect, and it had shocked me to leave Nur and John so suddenly. Everything seemed unreal. It took every effort of will not to turn around and go back to the village. Only when I had driven through the outskirts of London to Elizabeth could I, once more, begin to accept whatever was to be.

110

15

Elizabeth greeted me at the door in her usual manner, "Come on, now," she said. "In you come. The coffee's ready, and breakfast won't take a moment. Please forgive me for not being quite properly dressed yet." She was wearing a blue bathrobe and a pair of pink velveteen slippers with white pom-poms on the top. Her hair was tied back in the usual bun, and her monocle hung round her neck. "Sorry about the colors, dear," she said, sensing my thoughts, "but I find them rather fun. There's nothing like really bad taste for a giggle."

Over breakfast I told her all that I could recall, but it was hard to remember everything in the right sequence. Several times she stopped me and asked me to go over a conversation or a theme we had discussed, particularly those on the nature of time, conception, death, and the responsibility we have to commit ourselves to life once we have given ourselves to the Way.

"Whew!" she said finally. "All that in three days. You must be exhausted. But there you are. If you really want to know what life is all about, and the time is right, we can get picked right up from what we have been doing and dropped into the middle of a situation completely out of our depth. It's quite like that, isn't it?" she asked, smiling.

"Now, look, she said. "I have got certain things on today that I can't get out of. There's an emergency with some people I've promised to help, and I really can't let them down. There'll be time enough if we leave early tomorrow morning. You could rest in the guest room, if you like, or else go out for the day and we could meet for dinner in the city—but perhaps you have things to do at your flat?"

It was not difficult to realize that she did not want me around during the day. I was relieved, in fact, as I was really looking forward to having some time by myself. We agreed to meet at Sophie's that evening, and Elizabeth promised that she would be packed and ready to go in the morning.

"We must call Nur," she said after we had finished the dishes. "Why don't you get her on the telephone, and then I will speak to her or to John."

The telephone rang for a long time before there was any answer. "I'm sorry," Nur said on the other end, "I was upstairs with John."

"How is he?" I asked.

"He had a good night," she replied, "but he is still in a lot of pain. I have a funny feeling it is getting worse. If necessary, I'll call the doctor but otherwise, things are fine. When are you coming back?" I told her the arrangements that Elizabeth had made. She sounded sad and a little worried, but as soon as she and Elizabeth spoke it was obvious Nur was laughing again.

She's a wonderful woman, that Nur," Elizabeth said afterwards. "You must look after her. I imagine that neither of you have had much time this last week to consider yourselves nor where you are going. It's not surprising, but sooner or later the question is going to arise, isn't it? If you haven't put some energy into making a few plans, you could feel pretty much left in the lurch. Perhaps you could think about it today. Anyway, we'd better hurry. I've got to get myself ready for my guests. Call me in the afternoon just in case there have been any calls, and we can fix the exact time to meet at the bistro."

First I drove to my flat. There was a pile of letters on the floor but otherwise everything was the same as I had left it. So much had happened that, although things looked the same, they *felt* different and somehow foreign. I realized I had no need for half of the objects in the room, and I was sorely tempted to throw them out. But even that seemed a bit pointless and melodramatic. It was actually very hard to make any decision at all. Elizabeth had said that it was important to consider the future, but all I could think of was returning to Nur and John as soon as possible.

Being in London was a nightmare. The noise of the traffic, the cars in endless, crawling lines passed by on one side of the road—bumper to bumper, the grey suits, umbrellas, briefcases. I had been introduced to another world, and now I was facing what some people considered to be the only reality. I walked out from my flat towards Earls Court. The sound was deafening. Car horns, people shouting to one another. The pavement was swarming with people heading for the underground. It swallowed them up, figures disappearing into the earth to get home. Once I saw an old friend walking on the opposite side of the street. I couldn't face speaking to him and dodged into an alley so as not to be seen. Every impression seemed a hundred times stronger than before; the blaring of a taxi horn echoed in my head, making it impossible to think clearly. Even children calling to each other, sounds we normally take for granted, created a totally different impression from before. Finally I took a bus to Hyde Park. There were many quiet places there under the huge chestnut trees and somehow or other, I had to get adjusted to being back in London, even if only for a day.

I found a bench near the place Nur and I had watched the daffodils that day and witnessed that even the natural world responds to recognition in love. The flowers were still out, but their season was nearly over, and the brightness of the yellow was fading. I remembered the experience that we had had that day. It seemed so long ago now that it was almost unreal. I wondered what it would have been like if we had known then exactly what was to happen in the next week. I doubt if my mind could have absorbed the possibility of it.

The fact was that all the events had unfolded from that one moment in Konya when I had begun to experience what it meant to know I was loved. It was such an obvious statement, and although I must have known it all my life, I had never faced up to the consequences of what knowing this might mean. I began to wonder whether Nur had either.

The shock of coming back to London changed the time scale again. Old habit patterns emerged. The doubt and fear I had known before reappeared, making the experiences of the last few days seem flat and unreal. I remembered the many times I had sought agreement from others, protecting ourselves, in a sense, from facing our own fears and thus from taking any step in another direction. We thought we were being kind and helpful but it was just a sham.

I recalled what I had been told in Turkey. "What you are seeking is the Beloved—Truth—God—whatever words you wish to use. Therefore remind yourself always that you are moving from the world of appearances to the world of reality. You are moving from the world of form into the formless, until finally you may be able to say, without a shadow of doubt that 'God is Love, Lover, and Beloved.'"

London shocked me back into the past so strongly that I found my mind comparing everything. The possibility of understanding seemed as remote as the furthest mountain. For a while even Nur seemed unreal, and the past week like some sort of fairytale. Yet it *had* all happened: there was no denying it. Was my own doubt merely part of the "set-up"?

When I finally looked at my watch, I realized that I had been in the park for over three hours. My mind had gone round and round, so that it really made little difference whether I was awake or asleep. I rang Nur.

"What's the matter?' she asked when I finally got through to the cottage. "You sound different, is everything all right?"

"Everything down here seems so unreal," I complained. "I don't know what is and what isn't anymore. I seem to be doubting everything, and the noise of the streets is so deafening I can't think clearly. I've been in the park for hours. At one point, I was even wondering whether this past week was a dream. I'm only staying to see Elizabeth this evening or else I'd leave. I can't stand it here."

"You are in a state!" she said. "I know that one. For heaven's sake, don't just go on like that, wallowing in it. That just makes it worse. I wish I were with you. We could clear it up together. But I have John to look after. He seems a little better today and is sorting out masses of papers in his desk. Look, I'll tell you what to do, love. There are actually two ways that can help. Either you could go to a film and forget all about everything for a couple of hours, or else you could go back to the flat and really work with some of the practices that we have both learnt. Either way you'll have something to do. Call me this evening if you can."

But things just got worse. I could not imagine how to do anything creative, so I went to a film. The choice was about as stupid as the mood I had got myself into. It was a hackneyed plot about the break-up of a marriage, and it played it on every ounce of conditioned sentimentality and grief. From the reviews I had read in the newspaper, I thought it would be good but it was terrible. I stuck it out for a while and then left. There was still time to kill before meeting Elizabeth, so I called her to confirm the time as promised and then went back to my flat. Sick to death of the mood I had got myself into, I lay down and went to sleep. I couldn't even think about John. It was like living in a two-dimensional world.

Much later, I came to realize something that is stressed in transformation about regularity in practice. It's a simple idea, and quite obvious, but very easy to forget. If we are granted entry into the possibility of another way of life, we have an obligation to practice what we have been taught. In Elizabeth's words, "You have to go on so that illusions have no chance of creeping up, like weeding a garden. A bridge can be destroyed by the regularity of men stepping in perfect rhythm, and what we want is to be so regular in practice that 'false time' as John put it has no chance to get a hold."

Elizabeth and I had agreed to meet at a pub near the restaurant and she was already there when I arrived. "You've had a good day, I hope?" she asked. "What did you do?" My mood had lifted somewhat, but everything still felt displaced and meaningless. I did my best to explain while she listened patiently. Finally she interrupted, giving a huge wink. "You're too serious. Just when you are getting somewhere, you start thinking and look at the result. I did start the whole thing off, in a way, by asking you to look at the future, but that was necessary. What you have to learn is how to live in two worlds at once. By that I mean the world around us, the world of form, and the other world. They both need each other, don't you think?" Her face was perfectly noncommittal but I sensed she was teasing me. "After all, they are only separated so that you can see them more clearly. First you see one, then the other. When you really get it together, you will see that they are one and the same, just appearing differently.

"But enough. We've got dinner to eat. I get out so seldom it's a special treat. Just enjoy yourself, and the confusion will go."

Sophie's restaurant was a hive of activity that night. I had booked a table, which was lucky, as the place was packed. A Scottish folk group was playing, and the word had got round. Extra chairs had been brought in, and the waitresses were squeezing their way through the throng to serve food. It was a joyful evening. The group sang many early Scottish ballads, and everyone joined in the choruses. A piper came with them, the skirl of the bagpipes quickening a sense of courage and bravery that few other instruments can produce.

Sophie was her usual, happy self, greeting the guests at the tables, occasionally dancing a few steps with the group before returning to the kitchen to bring out another serving of borscht or boeuf Bourguignonne. Elizabeth and I sang with the rest.

"Don't worry, darlings, we'll have time to talk later," Sophie called.

Things quieted down around eleven o'clock. The group went on to another restaurant, and the guests were filtering out. I took the opportunity to call Nur and to say that things were fine again and that we would be leaving in the morning to arrive at John's by lunchtime if possible. Sophie came to sit with us.

"You didn't say you knew him," she said to Elizabeth, pointing at me. "You naughty woman, always keeping secrets from poor Sophie. What's he been doing this time, then?" They both laughed together, and then Elizabeth went on to tell her about Nur and me, and about John.

"I would like to see him again," said Sophie. "It's been a long time now. We have all been with the same school," she said to me," even if we don't speak of it. John, Sophie and others worked together in London more than twenty years ago. It was a time of great preparation. Now some of us are teachers, some are here, some there. Sophie runs a restaurant, but we are always together if we follow the Way. Isn't that right, darling?" she said, with her arm round Elizabeth. "When are you silly lady going to give up this piece of glass?" she said, picking up her monocle, "Sophie sees better out of her one eye without any glass!"

They burst into hoots of laughter, then, and it was so infectious that the remaining customers in the restaurant joined in.

"You mind your own business . . ." Sophie said, turning to them. "This is my business. You come again tomorrow and see me. That make Sophie very happy."

"You not worry, darling," she said to us. "Everything going to be fine. A play is a play, no?"

16

I left my flat about eight the next morning to collect Elizabeth for the drive to John's house. I had intended to leave early, but Elizabeth was still at her desk when I arrived and it looked as if she had been up all night writing. From the lines under her eyes I realized that she would be too tired to make the trip without stopping so I called Nur and explained the situation, saying that we would now be arriving sometime after lunch.

It was a beautiful day. Everything was fresh and green. The trees and hedgerows sparkled with life in the morning sunlight. Birds sang and chattered, darting in and out of the hedgerows by the side of the road and flew in flocks in front of the car, wheeling and circling. Small puffs of cloud scudded over the tops of the higher hills; otherwise, the sky was a deep blue. I remembered lying on the ground as a child looking up at such a sky, certain that I could see through it and still see the stars shining. The drive was calm and uneventful in spite of the confusion of the day before.

Elizabeth sat silently looking out of the window at the passing countryside. Her attitude that day was different. Gone was her usual brusque and funny manner; in many ways a mask hiding a deep, inner quality I had sensed but not seen. I did not disturb her, and it was she who eventually broke the silence.

"I have been dwelling on many things since yesterday," she said. "We have hardly had time to get to know each other. But when this cycle is completed I shall still be here, and perhaps there will be an opportunity for us to become more intimate. I realize how hard it must be for you and Nur to cope with the speed of events, but you see, none of us knew for certain the time of John's death. I am just as human in this as you are. It is not easy for me either to face the stark reality of this journey.

"You see, John has been more than a friend to me. We have been fellow pupils all these years, and we have had a very deep inner link. You must have seen this, but then I suppose that you and Nur have not had much time to talk about it. I have told her a few things about John's and my life together and how we were never able to be married. It has been a strange situation, for we committed ourselves from the very beginning, knowing that we could not share our lives together completely. Perhaps in some ways it has proved a good thing, but it has been at times very painful.

"John has always been right in the midst of life, in the centre of his own present moment. Some saw him "bigger than life," but that's so silly! How could anyone be bigger than what is? It is just that we live such poor lives half of the time, that people are envious of someone who knows the art of spontaneity.

"I love John deeply, for he taught me, little by little, that finally there is no separation. It is as though he is perpetually in touch with a vast storehouse of knowledge and energy. I believe that he finally tapped the source when he first became paralyzed. Perhaps the shock of the illness came as a gift at precisely the right moment.

"I am telling you these things because John taught me how to tap this source of life energy, and I hope that one day it will be available to you and Nur. The way, however, lies in commitment. I should be asking exactly what you and Nur are going to do, but it is difficult now. Just remember, that it is only through absolute commitment that you can be led, step-by-step, towards real freedom. The more we commit ourselves, the more each action we take affects everything else on this planet and thus the more responsible we have to be. Forgive me for being serious, but there is so much to be learned.

"We have to have a great deal of experience and knowledge to really help each other. This situation is ironic, for John and I always thought that it would be me who would go first. We talked about this over twenty years ago and studied ways to help someone through the transition of death. There is no real transition for John, for he has already come home. It will just be easing out of time into the timeless. If you commit yourself totally to the work of transformation, it could be the same for you. To die before you die, you must commit yourself totally to life, and then life itself becomes the guide and the teacher."

I knew of her deep concern for Nur and myself, and I realized her enormous discretion and her faith in the perfection lying within the matrix.

We drove on in silence. I was deeply affected by what Elizabeth had said. The road had been climbing steadily, and on a tall hill overlooking the River Wye in Herefordshire we found a country inn where we could stop for lunch.

Elizabeth got out of the car slowly. Her back was bent, and it was as if she was somehow older than the Elizabeth I had met in London. We went into the pub and sat by the open fire.

"What do you mean exactly by helping someone through death?" I asked her as the landlord brought us the sandwiches we had ordered. "What I'm trying to ask is whether there is anything special that we should know."

"No," she replied. "As I told you, it is somewhat different with John. It's very simple, really. You told your teacher that you wanted to know you were loved. There is a great key in that. You've understood a lot of it, but there are so many levels. For any of us to be free, there must be no attachments. Attachment is to do with time and space. We attach ourselves to things here, to people, memories, and so on because we are full of fear. We wonder what would happen if we had nothing to hold onto. Thus the different parts of our being hang on to the end—the physical body being the last to let go, for it is composed of the grossest matter. Fantastic as it sounds, even the cells in the body have a memory pattern.

"The body is a vehicle. We should respect it, for it is the home of the mind, but we should not get attached to it. In the same way, we should not identify with feelings and sensations. They, too, are vehicles for other, higher forms of energy. Thus I was taught "Energy follows thought." John has reached a state of non-attachment. He does not *think*, in the normal sense of the word, but uses pure thought, pure energy for inner work, both within himself and to help others. He is not attached to feelings, and yet that does not mean that he does not feel. Far from it! That man feels more deeply than anyone I have ever met. All of us in the school that we have been with for these many years were trained in the art of non-attachment. In death, that capacity is tested to the utmost. For John, now, it is only a matter of time. He is free in himself, but the life span of the body is not complete as yet.

"Forgive me for rattling on, but there is one thing I want to explain. A true master is able to choose the time of his death. The legends are full of incidents of those who knew the time and were completely conscious right up to, and through death itself. John knows perfectly well when this will be. We don't. He is master over his body and will know, at the right time, when it will let go. You are only beginning, so these matters may seem far beyond you, but it is all in the realm of possibility that you will come to understand. The fact is, you would not be here at this time if you had not already committed yourself to the Way. Now learn to commit yourself to life and to all the responsibilities 'down here' in this world, and you may find that life and the spiritual path are one.

"Come on. We must get going. Don't forget what I said about your own commitment and about Nur, for it is all part of what is going on at this time." She smiled at last, and waved her monocle at me. "Be sensible, but not too serious!" she said.

17

Nur came down the path to meet us. She must have seen the car arrive through the upstairs window. The three of us held each other very close. "Well," Elizabeth said finally. "We had better go in. It's strange to be here after so long."

Everything was quiet inside the house. Jim was in the hall. He had a stethoscope round his neck, and was just packing his bag. "You must be Elizabeth," he said, holding out his hand. "John has been talking about you all morning. He's not very well, I'm afraid, but that is to be expected. I have given him some medication to ease the pain, and I changed the dressing. He's in the upstairs room. I can't do anymore for the time being, but I'm sure he will be better when he sees you. Call me whenever you want."

"If you don't mind," Elizabeth said to us, "I would like to be alone with John for a while. I'll find my room later." She left her overnight bag by the door and went slowly upstairs. I heard John's door open and close.

Nur was radiant. I shall never forget that moment. It was as though we were meeting for the first time, all over again. We held hands; there were no words to speak. We kissed, and I knew, without any doubt, that I would ask her to marry me. This was the reality I sought. The pain, the confusion, the splitting of time, the pressure of those two short weeks vanished for a brief moment in the love that we had for each other and the love that permeated us both.

We held hands; I sensed that Nur understood. "Please—come and help me get the tea," she said. "We have work to do. There will be time to talk later."

I helped, and soon the tray was ready. "Shall I come up with you?" I asked.

"You'd better wait," she said. "I feel he will want to be alone with Elizabeth, so I shall just knock on the door and leave the tray outside."

The house felt strangely quiet and empty. I walked about from room to room, looking at the books and the objects on the table in the hall. Each one of them represented a section of John's life. Time stood still. It seemed an age until I heard her footsteps coming downstairs again.

"I was right," she said. "They want to be alone together, but John has asked us all to come up to be with him at suppertime. Come on; let's take our favorite walk by the river. He will be all right with Elizabeth there." She took my hand and we followed the path that led down to the pool by the bend of the river.

"When do you think it will be?" I asked finally. We had been sitting for a long time on the riverbank in silence. "Do you think tonight? Elizabeth said that people like John could choose the time of their own death. I feel incredibly nervous. So much is hanging in the balance. There are many things I want to say to you, but I just can't seem to . . . ."

"Shhh!" she said. "Just be quiet." She leaned over, put her hand over my mouth, and kissed my forehead. "How do we know? There is something that knows, though, and our job is just to be here for John, not to worry or to get agitated, or sad—none of these things. He's not worried. Ever since you left, he has been telling me that we must not fret. He told me last night how this was to be a joyous occasion. All he asked was that we be as awake and conscious as we could. Anyway, he said he wanted to talk to us about something more, so there may be time. Most important of all though, he reminded us not to be sentimental, for sentimentality, he said, is the greatest enemy of love. He actually told me that you were far too sentimental and that it was my job to help you. Come now," she said at the expression on my face, "we don't have much time together."

She lay down and closed her eyes. Her long hair flowed out across the grass. I lay beside her, sensing the beauty that expresses itself in the completion lying in woman. She was herself the womb of the moment. John had said that when something dies, something is conceived, ready to be born. The future unfolded itself in all its infinite possibilities. In that moment, for the first time in my life, the matrix was complete.

Back in the house after our walk, we busied ourselves with tidying up and getting the supper ready. Elizabeth's bag was still by the door, so I took it to her room. There were fresh flowers on the dressing table and a book of Mevlana's poetry by her bed. It was getting dark, so I drew the curtains and turned on the light by the side of her bed. The muffled sound of voices came from John's room, but otherwise everything was still. I went to our own room and looked out of the window. 'Darest thou now, O Soul, walk out with me toward the unknown region?' The words echoed round my head as I watched daylight fade from the hillside.

Nur and I sat downstairs quietly. She had finished in the kitchen, and we had time to speak while we waited for Elizabeth. "Nur, what really happened when I was away? I expected you to look tired and worried under all this strain. Instead, you look completely at ease."

She smiled. "Nothing much happened. John has been very weak and hasn't talked much. He has been busy with papers and notes and seemed to want to be left alone most of the time. Margaret came round once and called during the day, and that was about it, really."

"But there's something else. Something has changed in you. You seem gentler."

"Well, perhaps it is because I have completely accepted John's death," she answered. "It's all very well knowing that someone is being taken out of your life, but it is another thing to go with it. When we were alone together, it was not so much what he said that helped me but what he did not say. Sometimes after meals he asked me to sit with him; sometimes he talked, and sometimes he said nothing. When he did, he often spoke about you and me, and in a short time some inner confidence grew inside that I had lost a long time ago. Many things have happened since my illness, and there was a lot of mending to do. I suppose that when we are really confident in the moment there is no need to be agitated and nervous. That's about it, really," she said.

"What did John say about us?" I asked her.

"Oh, not too much. It was just a lot of personal things about man and woman and relationships. He extended what he had talked about before. You know, he said so much during those times, if you think about it, all those ideas about birth, sex, death and conception being in the same moment."

"But is there anything more specific that you could say about what he said? It does concern both of us."

"Well, to be quite honest," she said after a long while, "John implied that we should look at getting married. He can't understand why you haven't asked me." She got up and put another log on the fire. She had her back to me so I could not see her face.

There was still no sign of Elizabeth, and it was nearly suppertime. "Nur," I said, "did John really mean that?" She nodded silently.

"Do you wish to get married?" I asked her.

"Yes," she said quietly, "but only if you can accept this thing about destiny, that if there is total commitment we have to accept whatever life may bring. For me, marriage has to be a real commitment." She looked up at me then. Tears welled up in her eyes and fell down her face and ran over her lips. I had never seen the expression in her eyes in any woman before. This was the call for recognition, the longing to be accepted right down into the earth, into the flesh itself. I knew that she was not begging me to marry her, but that the longing in her eyes came from a deep part of woman herself, crying out to man to see and understand who she is and thus commit himself to the completion that is in woman. For a moment, we were caught in a bubble outside time, a split second lying between cycles. Then it was over. We held each other, and I asked her to marry me in the knowledge that we were committing ourselves not only to each other but also to life itself.

A few minutes later, we heard Elizabeth coming down the stairs. We must have looked very different, for she stopped for a moment and looked at us through her monocle. "Ah!" she said, warmly, "so there you are.

"John has asked that we all come up to his room now. I heard you moving about in the kitchen earlier on, so I guessed there's some food ready for us all. He doesn't want much, he says, perhaps a little soup if you have some. By the way," she said to me, "you haven't seen him for a couple of days. He is getting weaker all the time, so don't be surprised. He perked up quite a bit when I first came and we were able to talk about the old days, but he has been in and out of sleep most of the day, and I have just been sitting with him."

There was a marked change in John. He seemed thinner, as if a part of him were already gone. He was sitting in his chair. Nur brought him his soup and then sat down on a cushion by his feet. He smiled at us both, holding out his hand to me.

"It's already been a long time," he said.

He drank the soup silently. Eventually he turned to Nur. "Well?" he asked, "have you spoken with him?"

"Yes, John. We are going to get married. I haven't even told Elizabeth yet."

"Thank God!" he said. "Did you hear that, Elizabeth? Now all those things I saw so long ago are coming true at last. Ah, that's wonderful both of you. Come—look at me. Let us see if there is any change!"

"It is good," he said finally. "I think both Elizabeth and I saw that this might happen. It is a tremendous and wonderful decision. If I were only a little stronger, we would go out and celebrate. As it is, I can at least act as a sort of godfather for you both. I am very tired tonight, but perhaps tomorrow we can talk."

He leaned back in his chair. After a while he opened his eyes. "Don't speak now," Elizabeth said. "There is time enough tomorrow."

"You're right," he said. "But tonight you can meditate on one theme, one idea, and then tomorrow we will see what can be said. Just remember that you are not your bodies, you are not your senses or your emotions, and you are not even the mind that you call yours. You are none of these things, and yet the body is the vehicle through which everything comes into being here, in this world. Thus, as marriage is sacred, so are your bodies. In Love, there is nothing that is not sacred. Every one of the manifestations of God is sacred, and they are all contained within you. Marriage is a wonderful gift, for through it you can free God. Think of it. God is love and love is pure energy, from which everything becomes. All this is locked inside the prison of the body, of the mind and of the senses. Marriage is for the freeing of love into the world, whether it is the marriage within, or the outward expression of this when two people agree to be united. We are united in love but God is still imprisoned with the illusions we have created for ourselves. Free God, both of you! Free the love that is within you. Each of you is a mirror for the other; each of you can be a help to the other towards the only true freedom that there is. For me, at last, there is nothing left but God."

That night we did not sleep. Something irreversible had been put in motion in the decision we had made and in what John had said to us afterwards.

18

Dawn came in a clear sky. We heard John moving about, and then his door opened. The sound of the wheels on his chair stopped outside our door, and he knocked very quietly. "Come," he said, "we do not want to wake Elizabeth. She is tired and needs rest.

"This is the best time of all," he said to us. "Now things can be heard in quite a different way. Push me over to the desk. There is something I want to give you both."

Bundles of papers were neatly stacked in piles on the desk, and in the middle of them was a small box.

"This is a seal that I was given many, many years ago. I want to hand it on to you. It was given to me in trust, and it is your turn to have it. One day you must give it to someone else. Here, take it!"

He handed us the box. Nur opened it. Inside was a roughly carved bronze seal. There were no words on it, just the picture of a sikke, the tall hat worn by the dervishes who follow the way of Mevlana.

"You understand this," he said to me. Turning to Nur, he said, "The meaning is simple. The dervishes wear this hat depicting the tombstone to mean that they have already died to the illusions before they cast off the body. The word *dervish* literally means "threshold." One day I pray you both will be real dervishes for those who will come after you.

"Now, then," he said, "there are a few more things to say. Please just listen. Allow yourselves to hear the inner meaning of what I am saying. The meaning is not limited by a number of letters formed into words. It is the inner meaning I want to transmit.

"By now you know, I am sure, that we have all been travelling the same road, knowingly or not. I have hinted at this when I said to you at the very beginning that it was in the way of Mevlana that I saw the ultimate possibility. I am not saying that it cannot be found in other ways. Of course it can, for there *is* only Love. But it is kismet that brought us together on the same path, and through this path we are granted the possibility of seeing how everything is moving toward completion. It is said that Mevlana reached union with God, but what could this mean, in the light of what I said to you last night? Surely it would be that there was nothing that stood between the truth and the manifested world. In those days, when the structure of religion was so clearly defined, could you imagine what effect this man had on the world? Is there a difference now? Has God ceased to wish to be free?

"Perhaps the most famous of all Mevlana's words are these:

Come, come, whoever you are,
Wanderer, worshipper, lover of leaving,
It doesn't matter.
Ours is not a caravan of despair.
Come, come even if you have broken your vows a thousand times.
Come—come yet again, come.

"Have these words as the motto of your life together. Once the door of your heart has been opened, you may never again close it. Christians, Jews, and Moslems have the same God, so receive all those who come to you. Help free the God in them, as you will help to free the God in each other. Help them understand, whomever they are, that it is only through total commitment in everything that we do that we can serve this imprisoned God. Look into the motive and intention behind your actions and study the purpose of life. Be clear in your intention so that your motive is pure. Learning is unending; the answer manifesting in every moment, burning away the veils until there is no more 'you' and 'I', but only this vast Unity in all life remaining. Never underestimate yourselves, for if you do you will again lock the door of the prison. The God in each of you is equal, for there is only One. Let this be the theme of your marriage and your life together.

"There is one other thing," he said, "and then I need to rest for a while. On the desk over there are three books containing the six volumes of the *Mathnawi* by Mevlana Jalalu'ddin Rumi. It is considered by those of the Way to be one of the great mystical books in the Sufi tradition. If you know how to read it, you will find the answers to your questions. Accept that which is said in it is true. Here, hand them to me."

Nur went over to the desk and brought them back to John. "Read a little every day," he said. "Contemplate on the meaning in what you have read. Today I will read for you."

We watched as he took the three books, and then, with his eyes closed, chose one and opened it at random. He read:

"'When the candle is wholly naughted in the fire of Divine Illumination,

128

you will not see any trace of the candle or the rays of its light.

"'This is the everlasting radiance, and that bodily candle is perishable; the candle of the Spirit hath a Divine flame.'

"So you see, conscious death is nothing more than releasing the everlasting fire of the Spirit."

He handed the books to us. "I'm very tired now," he said, "but please, could you ring Margaret and ask if she would come round to see me in a couple of hours?"

The day passed like a dream. We made breakfast for Elizabeth, but none of us ate very much. She saw the seal and the copy of the Mathnawi but did not say anything. Margaret came to visit John around eleven. She stayed for a short time, and then we saw her walking quietly down the stairs and out through the front door. She did not turn her head. Jim called at lunchtime and spoke with Elizabeth, and then she went upstairs. The house was very quiet.

No one said anything. It felt as though the slightest sound would break the space, interrupting the timeless, patient wait between a man and his destiny. We were all experiencing it. I found myself walking about, doing odd jobs in the house, unable to settle. Nur was sitting in the garden. About four o'clock, I heard the gate open, and I walked out quickly to ask whomever it was to come back another day. It was an old man I had never seen before. He stood there watching the house. He looked like a gardener or someone who worked in the fields. His boots were caked with mud, and his trousers and jacket were worn with age, as was the faded green hat he wore on his head. As I walked up to him, he put his finger to his hat and took out an incredible rose from the basket he was carrying. Its colour was so deeply red that the inner petals seemed like black velvet. He handed it to me and pointed to the upstairs window. Then he turned quietly and walked down the lane. I never saw him again.

Not long afterwards, Elizabeth came out to fetch us and I forgot the rose I had been given.

"It will not be long now," she said. "He wants you to come in." Her voice was full, and I saw that her eyes were brimming with tears.

Nur and I climbed the stairs slowly. I tried to remember what John had taught me: "Keep your intention before you with every step you take. You wish for freedom, and you must never forget it."

The door was ajar, and a shaft of sunlight spread out lighting the top of the stairs. John's voice was weak, but there was no trace of fear or sadness in it.

"Come in," he said.

Somehow or other, Elizabeth had moved him to his bed. The sheets had been newly changed, and he was propped up high so that he could see through the window and out across the fields toward the hills. It looked as though less than an hour of sunlight remained. Already shadows were forming across the lawn, and the sun was moving toward the trees at the end of the garden.

"Don't be afraid. Come, get chairs and sit close to me." Nur and I sat on one side of the bed, and Elizabeth on the other. He was very pale, and his breath was sporadic. The wound was covered with gauze, and you could see the veins throbbing, moving the gauze a little each time. He had his inevitable pipe burning away in the ashtray beside him.

"I don't have to worry about the habit much longer." We laughed, and then his voice became serious.

"You know," he said, "we come into life on the breath, and we go out on the breath. It is His Breath of Compassion that brings us into the world and it is the same breath that takes us into the world of reality that lies here, all the time. Do you understand? I want so much that you understand."

"Yes," I said. "Somewhere I do know."

"Let us breathe together for the time we have. Both of you have brought me so much joy, for you have been able to take on much that I have been given, and now it is up to you to pass this knowledge on to others. Never forget that the future of this planet lies in the hands of the children. We are chosen by them. If you are both open to this, you may be granted a child that will carry this line of knowledge into a waiting world."

There was so much that I wanted to ask him, and so many things that I wanted to apologize for, but I had to catch myself and remember that this time was all the time we had, that death and conception are in the same moment, and so it would be in silence that something new would be born.

"Don't be sad." His voice faltered for a moment, and he started coughing violently. Nur wiped his forehead with a cool cloth until the spasms died down. I noticed that there was moisture in the palms of his hands and spreading out from his neck through the simple vest he wore. The sun was low.

"It isn't necessary to be sad," he said, turning slowly to Elizabeth. "There is mourning in the time of transition, but remember, I have nothing to take with me but the knowledge of love. I do not need anything any more. There is nothing to search for at last." Making one great effort he reached and took our hands in his.

Something changed in the room. The pressure mounted. Sweat broke out on my forehead; tears were running down Elizabeth's face. Nur was quite quiet. John looked at us each in turn, deep into our eyes. He looked so deeply into them that it was as though he was looking through them, as one would look through a window. The grip on his hands became tighter, and I noticed

130

that I could see the reflection of the setting sun in his eyes. His head was bathed in the last, orange-pink rays of light.

"It is time. Breathe with me," he said quietly. "Don't turn away."

Suddenly his body started shaking, ripples that passed through every muscle and fibre. I could see he was in great physical pain, yet he was so completely conscious he was beyond the pain. We held his hands as we watched the glistening light in his eyes start to fade. The light of the sunset moved slowly down his face and across the sheets over his chest. For a moment, our hands were bathed in it.

The room was very still. His voice was so faint now that we were leaning forward to be able to hear what he was saying. Then, with a great shudder, his body moved onto the right side and I saw the blood. The artery had burst in his shoulder. It poured out onto the bed. With his eyes, he signaled us not to do anything. Using the last of his strength, he moved his head so that he could see through the open window. The blood moved on, a spreading red river. We turned to look with him. The sky had turned red in the sunset. The first star shone over the top of the pine tree. The last bird had ceased its calling.

"I love you," he said. "There is nothing else."

We stayed with him until it was dark, and then Elizabeth gently closed his eyes. Nur went down and got the rose we had been given from the kitchen and put it in a vase beside the bed . . . its perfume filled the room. Nur put her arm round Elizabeth, and they moved silently out of the room.

I was alone with John now. It was a timeless state, yet containing all time within it. He had said that death and conception were the same moment. I had never totally understood this, but in the quiet of that room its truth was beginning to dawn on me. How foolish to be sentimental about death! Sentiment and Love are the greatest enemies, and if Love is the cause of creation, and Love is its own effect, so the manifestation of Love in the form of a child comes through something apparently dying. Yet truly there is no death, and when I looked out through the open window with John in those last moments I knew this, not just as theory, but as a living reality, from the knowledge of which I could now never escape. Nor would I want to. The journey of the soul on the path of return is not a sentimental journey. That is what the mind would like to make it in order to protect itself and the illusions it creates. The real journey of the soul is a journey within the spirit itself, a journey outside of time.

Nur came back into the room. "It is time to go," she said. "Jim will be here soon, and Elizabeth wants us to go to Margaret and tell her it's over." Nur arranged the bedclothes neatly and then covered them all with a clean bedspread. Bending down, she kissed John's forehead, and then, without turning

131

back, left and went down the stairs.

I followed her out into the garden. Taking flashlights with us, we walked silently over to Margaret's house.

RESHAD FEILD - BIOGRAPHY

The life story of Dr. Reshad Feild reads like a modern-day Odyssey propelled by the single question, *"What is the purpose of life on earth?"*

Reshad, whose original name was Richard Timothy Feild, was born in England in 1934 where he received a formal education, typical of the upper classes at that time. He first went to boarding school at the age of 8, and then on to Eton College until he joined the British Navy when he was 18 years old. After two years in the Navy his mystical yearning took him around the world on his first major quest. Perhaps he was one of the very early "spiritual hippies" of his time. He learned to play the guitar and sang his way to the States, singing in a second-class bar on the liner, *The Queen Mary*. In fact he sang his way around the States, traveling from place to place, and finally landed in Japan where he spent some time in a Zen monastery before moving on to Thailand and India. However, he always says that his first major breakthrough in his spiritual journey was when he was way up in the Himalayas, on the borders of Afghanistan, where he met a group of dervishes and was first introduced into the mystical world of the Sufis. He was then only 21 years old, but he became very ill and had to return to his native England.

From then onwards his life's journey unfolded with an almost relentless momentum. He worked in the daytime in London, but became a singing waiter in the evenings for Madame Luba, the niece of the great G.I. Gurdjieff, perhaps one of the most controversial figures in the mystical tradition over the past 100 years. He also attended the esoteric schools involved with the Sufi Path of Universal Love, continuing with his studies and travels in his search for the essence of all religious and mystical teachings throughout time.

During the time with Madame Luba, Tim, as he was then known, was spotted by a show business promoter, and within a year he had helped start what became the most famous pop/folk group of its time. The band was called *The Springfields*, and consisted of Tim, Dusty Springfield, and her brother Tom. The group triumphed in those days and received the award of the Best Vocal Group of 1963. Dusty then went on to pursue a solo career, remaining one of the most loved and respected singers in the West until her death some years ago. Tom retired from the public eye, and Tim went on to become an antique dealer and interior designer in London. The first of his three sons was born at that time.

It was during his career as an antique dealer that Tim, soon to be renamed *Reshad*, met his spiritual teacher in London. A great deal of the story of this meeting and the journeys which followed are illustrated in Reshad's first book, *The Last Barrier*, although, as Reshad said, it would take more than the many books he wrote over the years to tell the full story! He often says that if he had told everything that happened during the first years with Hamid, the name he gave for his teacher in the book, no-one would have got past the first chapters! The journey of a thousand miles may start with one step, but no-one ever tells the seeker after Truth what that journey might entail, what endless sacrifices might have to be made, and the patience and perseverance necessary on what is, after all, what the late Somerset Maugham called *The Razor's Edge*. Truth is not necessarily glamorous!

Until September, 1973, Reshad was based in England where he helped start a very large International Center based on the essence of Sufi Teachings, which continues to this day in Scotland. However, to Reshad's surprise, in the Fall of that year, his teacher then sent him to Canada and the States, to start further Centers, and continue to give the inner teachings. For 15 years he traveled throughout the States, Canada, and Mexico, before returning to Europe where he brought together people from all over the world for a period of intense training in the inner traditions of the spiritual journey in another Center in Switzerland. The Center was disbanded in 1994.

Reshad has written many books, many of which are published in several languages. He continues to teach and divides his time between New Mexico and Europe. Although he says that his teachings and the methods he gives to his students are based on the essence of Sufi Teachings, he prefers to have no label himself. He states, *"We are just People of the Way,"* and often quotes the great 13th century Sufi Master Ibn el Arabi who said, *"The wise man follows no set form or belief, since he is wise unto himself."*

134

Dear Reader of *To Know We're Loved,*

If you have enjoyed reading this book, you may also appreciate other titles in our Consciousness Classics series.

We at Gateways Books and Tapes have now, for almost thirty years, brought to you the finest spiritual and esoteric classics, which are otherwise very hard to find. Our promise to you is that we will continue to make available to you, our esteemed reader, a selection of the finest consciousness-related writings of our times.

For a current catalog and referral to related books and study materials, you may contact Gateways at the address below with no obligation to purchase.

Reshad Feild's published books include:

The Last Barrier
The Invisible Way
Going Home
Steps to Freedom
Here to Heal
The Alchemy of the Heart
Breathing Alive
and others.

He can be contacted through Gateways Books & Tapes or at:
www.Chalice.net

Gateways Books and Tapes
P.O. Box 370-TK
Nevada City, CA 95959
(800) 869-0658 or (530) 272-0180
www.gatewaysbooksandtapes.com
email: info@gatewaysbooksandtapes.com

A Partial List of Titles You Can Order
(See www.gatewaysbooksandtapes.com for complete current book list)

by Robert S. de Ropp
The Master Game: Pathways to Higher Consciousness
Self-Completion: Keys to a Meaningful Life
Warrior's Way: A Twentieth Century Odyssey

by Reshad Feild
To Know We're Loved
Alchemy of the Heart (forthcoming)

by E.J. Gold
American Book of the Dead
The Great Adventure: Talks on Death, Dying and the Bardos
The Human Biological Machine as a Transformational Apparatus
Practical Work on Self
The Hidden Work
The Seven Bodies of Man
Visions in the Stone: Journey to the Source of Hidden Knowledge
   (Intro. by Robert Anton Wilson)

by John C. Lilly, M.D.
The Deep Self (due in 2004)
with E. J. Gold: *Tanks for the Memories*

by Claudio Naranjo, M.D.
Character & Neurosis: An Integrative View
The Divine Child and the Hero: Inner Meaning in Children's Literature
The Enneagram of Society (due in 2004)

by Reb Zalman Schachter-Shalomi & Howard Schwartz
The Dream Assembly

by Ka-Tzetnik 135633
Shivitti: A Vision

by Dr. Claude Needham, Ph.D.
The Original Handbook for the Recently Deceased